W9-ATE-295

CREATING
CHILDREN'S
SERMONS

BROWN MEMORIAL
WOODBROOK PRESBYTERIAN
CHURCH - LIBRARY

CREATING CHILDREN'S SERMONS

51
Visual
Lessons

by
BUCKY DANN

899

THE WESTMINSTER PRESS
Philadelphia

Copyright © 1981 The Westminster Press

All rights reserved—no part of this book may be
reproduced in any form without permission in
writing from the publisher, except by a reviewer
who wishes to quote brief passages in connection with a review in magazine or newspaper.

BOOK DESIGN BY DOROTHY ALDEN SMITH

First edition

Published by The Westminster Press®
Philadelphia, Pennsylvania

PRINTED IN THE UNITED STATES OF AMERICA
9 8 7 6 5 4 3 2 1

Library of Congress Cataloging in Publication Data

Dann, Bucky, 1951–
    Creating children's sermons.

    Includes index.
    1. Preaching to children. 2. Children's sermons—
Outlines.   I.Title.
BV4235.C4D36   251   81–10493
ISBN 0–664–24383–5   AACR2

For Rachel and Jesse
my most special children

CONTENTS

LESSONS

THE NATURE OF GOD

THE NATURE OF JESUS

EVIL

THE ATONEMENT

THE TEACHINGS OF JESUS

DISCIPLESHIP

THE MEANING OF CHRISTMAS

PALM SUNDAY

INTRODUCTION

Some of my clearest childhood memories are of X-rated Sunday mornings. Sunday morning may seem a strange time to find X-ratings. But the fact is, both our worship service and the minister were intended for adults only. I was not included, as a child, in either the Sunday worship or the pastor's personal care. Worship was a time to draw on bulletins; the minister was the man up front who shook my hand as I left.

Worship services are barometers for congregations. They reveal the theology, the spirituality, and the interpersonal feelings that exist in each local church. In the same manner, they indicate how each church ministers to children. Unfortunately, in my experience, Sunday morning reveals that children are excluded from the body of Christ. They are shut out physically, emotionally, and spiritually by poor communication. Whatever a church does in worship, evangelism, Bible study, or pastoral care, its focus is unmistakably on adults. Children are simply excluded from most forms of ministry and clergy care. My childhood experience is not unusual.

This preoccupation with adults is understandable. Adults do the work of the church; they contribute the money to support its program and carry its influence into society. But this preoccupation leads the church away from an explicit command of Christ.

Jesus Christ gave children a special place in his ministry.

Scolding his disciples for preventing some children from coming to him, Jesus took those children in his arms, placed his hands on them, and blessed them. Then he affirmed their importance. "Let the children come to me, do not hinder them; for to such belongs the kingdom of God. Truly, I say to you, whoever does not receive the kingdom of God like a child shall not enter it." (Mark 10:13–16.) By example and teaching, Christ commands his followers to minister to the needs of children. He speaks against the notion that only adults are important. His statements, in fact, exalt children.

Despite his seeming idealism, Jesus was a practical thinker. His injunctions were often filled with great usefulness, meeting needs on many levels. This is true of his love for children. His command reflects an overriding concern for the little ones of society. At the same time, it reveals a concern for his church's strength and growth.

One reason for Christ's command is obvious. Children represent the future of the church. They are the developing members of Christ's body; the depth of their spiritual commitment will greatly affect the body's future health. They will replace us. They will deal with the problems and tragic possibilities that we fearfully foresee. Childhood is the time to lay spiritual foundations, to establish respect for the Bible's meaningfulness, and to recognize the church's usefulness.

Spirituality begins in childhood, as Jesus knew. A child's spiritual foundations are laid even when the child receives no particular ministry. A positive church experience in which a child is involved, taught, and appreciated will be drawn upon later in adult life. A pastor who is accessible to children and supportive of them will leave a lasting impression on them about the ministry and the church. Providing a positive experience becomes a major responsibility of the congregation.

However, the church is often reticent, like parents who don't discuss sexuality with their child. Withholding from children what they should be taught leaves them to learn what they can in other places. Our society is constantly communicating messages about love, power, and redemption that are quite different from the Christian message. This results in prevalent confusion about the meaning of love, the nature of God, and the source of our redemption. Since so many children are not actively included in worship and pastoral care, it is no wonder that the young come to regard religion as a separate compartment in life. What happens on Sundays deals with the afterlife, with little practical relevance to daily living. The children's ties to the church are most often tenuous.

The adult belief that a child's abilities are greatly limited restricts ministry to children. Doctrines and ideas are not taught to them. Communion is withheld. Children are not allowed to participate in worship. The pastor neglects them. Compounding this problem is the inability of many adults to communicate with children. The adults are unable to relate to the feeling plane in which children live: awe, mystery, fantasy, playfulness.

This culminates in children whose church experience is negative, whose spiritual foundations are shallow. Pastors wait, like the disciples, until children are old enough to understand, or old enough to benefit from pastoral care. Children are taught simplicities that leave them bored. They are regarded as disturbers of worship. Sometimes they are even forbidden to enter the sanctuary. The result is more than the poor spiritual development of a child; it is the retardation of an entire Christian life, even generations of lives. The neglect of children in worship undermines the church's future.

This need not be. Children understand more and are capable of learning more than many adults believe possible. They can be taught about the atonement, Christology, prayer, the church, and love. They are able to discuss death, God, and the Spirit. I have had children pray publicly during Sunday worship and receive Communion with reverence. Early in life they can learn the Christian equivalent of an alphabet and tying shoes. Mastering more of the Christian life as they grow, they build upon their first foundations. They can have a relationship with Christ as a child, and find the church to be a meaningful part of their life.

Christ's command concerning children is also more than a matter of church growth. Christ offers a healing message for children which every child needs to hear.

Childhood years are formative years. Decisions that children make can easily affect the rest of their life. Psychiatrists spend their professional careers trying to help adults overcome bad experiences they had as children. These are years when the Christian gospel must be communicated.

Children must face life's realities without the assistance of a developed system of beliefs. They are confronted with the limitations of their body and with their sheer dependence on others. They are filled with anxiety and fear, clearly aware of their smallness and weakness. Not surprisingly, children often conclude that something is wrong with them, and they suffer through life with a poor self-image. Cultural forces bear down upon a child's natural openness, willingness to love, ability to trust, and sense of truth. These same forces instill feelings of unworthiness and fears of love.

Children need the protection of the gospel. Their fears, their feelings of pressure from overwhelming forces, their poor self-image can be relieved by hearing the Christian message. Christ reaches out to prevent children from being crushed by their own society. Taking children in his arms, holding them, and blessing them, Jesus knew their importance, and their vulnerable and fragile natures. We should learn from Jesus! Children need ministry; they need to be taken aside and made to feel special. They need to know they are accepted, important, and lovable. No minds are more open or hearts more willing to believe than those of children in their struggle with the terrors and imponderables of life. It is blindness to concentrate only on adults when children are a mission field in our own churches.

Many aspects of church life can be utilized to fulfill our ministry with children. Sunday school is the most frequently used form of child ministry, although its potential is far from reached. Bible study, fellowship, and caring groups for children can also be used. I lead a caring group for children who are in grades two through six. Churchwide family programs with a content attractive to children, such as puppet shows and cartoons, can also be planned.

Perhaps most important is to involve children in the morning worship service. In the church I serve we have a children's choir, and a children's sermon with a special Scripture reading. The children come to the front of the church, which allows me to relate to them more closely. The special time makes it possible to communicate with them on their level, and to include elements in the worship service meaningful and enjoyable for them.

In Sunday school, Bible study, or worship a children's lesson provides an opportunity for teaching the Christian message and its meaning. It offers a chance to establish friendships with the children. It may also open opportunities for pastoral care. A children's lesson, when done well, can be a highly effective tool for children's ministries. Children's sermons or lessons deserve to receive more time and effort than is commonly spent on them.

Once while I was teaching children a Bible lesson about the atonement, the moment came when the full impact of Christ's offering was comprehended and the children began spontaneously to cheer and applaud. Christ had become meaningful for their life.

That experience fueled my interest and concern. Perhaps there is reason to hope that an intentional ministry with children may bring about a deeper impact and truly life-changing results as children are influenced during the years of life-forming decisions. In adulthood change takes place at those precious junctures in life when a living situation has cracked a person open and before the shell can be snapped shut once more. In childhood the shell is not yet fully constructed. It is a tragedy to neglect those malleable years and struggle only with the hardened shell of later lives.

Children can develop strong spiritual foundations; they can be active members of Christ's church. Children can be led to Christ and to his healing touch. The lessons suggested in this book are efforts to enter into the children's land as we attempt to speak a special language to a special people.

Goals

Peter Marshall once said, "I am growing more and more aware that all too often we preachers (and teachers) aim at nothing and hit it." He pinpoints a common fault. Lessons that accomplish little probably had little to accomplish. An effective message for children will have conscious goals based upon an awareness of children's needs and abilities.

Education is always intentional. There is much to be learned in the small amount of time a church has with its children. Knowing this, we must plan to teach as effectively as possible, using a knowledge of how children learn. Set a personal goal, in nearly every lesson, to provide a means by which the message will be visualized or experienced in an elemental way.

Every aspect of the Christian message can be used in choosing what to teach. Do not shortchange the children by underestimating their ability to understand or to deal with reality. Death is a significant and acceptable subject. Children have faced it through the death of pets, if not of a family member. They have many questions. The atonement is not too abstract or difficult for children. In fact, it neatly fits their experience of the world. If you employ the full spectrum of Christian beliefs, you will always have a variety of themes to deal with and you can provide the children with a broad background.

The gospel also has a healing message which touches upon a child's personal needs. Let this goal be as important as education. Plan to influence children's developing self-image with Christ's uplifting teachings. "Love your neighbor as you love yourself." It is good to love yourself. Teach children that; help them do it. Communicate how special and important they are, to you and to the Lord.

Beyond the theme, use the lesson time as a chance to offer caring support. Permit the children to experience Christian love and acceptance in you. When children are open and willing to share their experiences, support them. If there is an opportunity to express physical affection, do it. One touch is sometimes worth a thousand loving words. When they try to understand, or answer questions, congratulate them for their effort. Thank them for being involved. A common goal in every lesson is to lift the children up, express care, be a friend. Plan to love them. A lot of raw material goes into their personal development; every ounce of acceptance and love is soaked up. It will fall into many a child's vast emptiness.

Use the studies also to help children develop spiritual skills. Prayer, for example, is important for all Christians, including young ones. A child who can talk can pray, and does. Teach children about prayer and pray with them. Familiarize them with the Bible: the Old and New Testaments, the different types of books, chapter and verse numbers. Encourage their reading and let those who can read with you.

Having fun is also an appropriate goal. Some adults would discount this as lacking in seriousness or real accomplishment. But that would be a wrong conclusion. Children's time should be a good time, relaxed, with the children able to be themselves. Church can be enjoyable and interesting. A positive, happy experience communicates to all children regardless of age or interest, even if the specific message is lost on them. Because of a child's short attention span, best results come when the lesson is entertaining and moves along.

All these goals can be present in every lesson. Each one deals with different facets of a person. Certain goals will be accentuated, either purposely or spontaneously, in each lesson. But the goals work well together and minister to the whole child. Spiritual foundations will be established, and the children will receive a pastoral ministry.

When these educational and personal goals are brought together with an expression of Christ's love, they lead to the highest goal. Children will personally meet Jesus Christ. A child can invite Christ into his or her heart, a decision freely made and made responsibly. Nothing is more important. Jesus will enter that child's life and will remain for eternity.

Technique

Abandonment. Imprisonment. Cannibalism. Most people wouldn't include these themes in a lesson for children. Nevertheless, they are the subject matter of "Hansel and Gretel." This fairy tale has enduring appeal because of its themes, not in spite of them. The Brothers Grimm understood a child's mind, and so their storytelling works. The lesson for us is to use what communicates with children, which may be quite different from what one would think.

It is important to determine how goals with children can effectively be accomplished. With the amount to be done and the shortness of time, effectiveness is especially essential. Employ methods carefully to avoid wasting your time and opportunities. Continually ask yourself if the goals were achieved. If not, why not? Was there real communication, or just a preacher talking? What was communicated? Avoid the trap of believing that children respond to sentimental themes spoken in "little people" talk. If the Brothers Grimm had believed that, "Hansel and Gretel" never would have been written. What appears childlike does not necessarily work well.

In developing technique, it is helpful to know how children think and perceive the world. Even more helpful is knowing how they learn. Experience and observation are the fundamental dynamics. Children learn more by watching than they do by listening. They learn more from what they experience than from what they are told. These twin insights must inform any children's lesson. This means that the focus will be upon demonstration. In some manner the message must be taken beyond the level of lecture and be objectified in the child's awareness by visualization or opened to the child's experience. Without this, the message will remain abstract and less effective.

Begin by distilling the major point into a simple sentence, with simple words. The theme, when pronounced to the children, should be short and clear. Break down the message until it is simply worded and brief. This practice helps you to know what you want to say. It will also be a statement easily repeated several times during the lesson, giving the children many opportunities to hear and understand.

A clear, concise theme also makes demonstration possible. Find a prop, a trick, or a game that conveys the thought, or even carries the burden of the message. What you use, too, should be simple. Props are less effective if they are complicated or contrived. Games are less effective if they require much explanation. The demonstrations are meant to communicate plainly without words.

A good example of the use of props is the lesson "The Candle That Won't Go Out." The theme: Easter celebrates the day Jesus came back to life. The demonstration: a trick birthday candle that relights after being blown out. The candle transmits the meaning of resurrection and can be the center of the lesson. It gives a visual message, enabling the children to learn by observation. As well, it adds color and action, which makes the lesson interesting and much more fun.

Games utilize the dynamic of experience. Also, they are fun and allow children to participate actively. The lesson "Jesus Says" uses the game Simon Says to teach about obedience to Christ. Playing the game, children experience the meaning of obedience and of disobedience.

When the educational message is demonstrated it makes abstractions concrete, and expresses them in terms children can readily grasp. Even when children cannot comprehend the explanations, they will remember the demonstrations. The demonstrations become physical parables of the theme.

Observation and experience are also important for accomplishing the personal, caring goals. God's love for children must be communicated by more than words. What do children observe along with the words? What do they feel from the teacher or preacher? A lesson about God's love can be vitiated by a person who says the right words, but acts withdrawn. It is self-negating to act aloof while describing Christ's warmth, especially with children, who by nature are very perceptive.

When working with children, forget you are a preacher or a teacher. Be a friend, a loving person, a child speaking through an adult who understands. Do not try to be some distant voice of God. Be warm, affectionate, inviting, and interested in them. Treat them like the important church members they are. Allow Christ to love the children through you.

These methods are to be linked with dialogue. A children's lesson cannot be effective if communication goes only one way. Involve the children in discussing the message. Ask them questions; let them talk about their thoughts and situations. A three-year-old has a lot to say, if the child feels safe and invited.

This interaction allows you to learn about events in the children's lives: their fears, needs, joys, disappointments, and desires. Listen between the words to what is happening inside. Look for those children who lack confidence, who are insecure, or who cannot say anything good about themselves. Dialogue offers excellent opportunities to support their sharing, congratulate their achievements, or reward desired behavior. It can be used to build them up and communicate acceptance.

This lesson process will create friendships with the children as they share themselves. It is perfectly appropriate to share yourself in return; to share your own embarrassing moments. A story about the day I locked the baby-sitter out of the house is one that children love. The personal relationships may be of more value than teaching doctrine.

It is assumed, for these lessons, that the children will be gathered together. Only in a gathering will all of them be able to see the demonstrations or play in the games. Dialogue will be impossible if the children are spread across a room or separated by pews in a sanctuary. Gathered together in worship, the children have a special time just for them, ahead of everyone else, alone with their pastor.

It is also important to include Scripture in these lessons. Children must know that the Bible is for them too. They may not immediately grasp the meaning, but they will know that the Bible is part of their special time. Keep the reading short. Use a translation, such as the *Good News Bible,* which has simple, common vocabulary. (All the readings for the lessons in this book came from the *Good News Bible.*) Longer Scripture passages may be used if the children can read for themselves, aloud. Children enjoy using their reading skills. Reading aloud also keeps them involved in the passage, reading and following, and helps the leader know what words and concepts give the children difficulty.

The lesson should not be long. In a worship service, seven to ten minutes is manageable. In a Bible study, thirty to forty minutes can be used, if well planned. Keep the lessons moving. Do not let them drag into a fading discussion that trails off the subject. A child's mind that has also trailed away with the discussion is harder to regain.

Storytelling is a category unto itself. It does not fit well into the criteria I use for technique. Storytelling offers little experiencing, little dialogue and interaction. As it is usually done, storytelling is one-way communication, with the danger that children will take a mental vacation. Many people use stories with children, but do not do them well. Storytelling is an art which has few remaining artists.

Yet a productive, powerful story immerses children in the story's little world. A child's imagination is stimulated, and storyteller and listener are brought together. The storyteller is part actor, part listener. If the story is done well, morals are not necessarily needed. The story may be left to distill in the child's mind.

These techniques are meant to educate and minister to children. They offer the potential to teach, heal, and build relationships in each lesson. They also give opportunity to lead children to meet Jesus Christ. In appropriate situations, I have found it meaningful to offer children opportunities to ask Christ into their life through prayer. I do not leave it as an abstract request. I give them specific choices: Ask Jesus to be their friend, ask Jesus to come into their hearts and stay with them forever, or ask Jesus to forgive all they have done wrong. I instruct the children to pray silently if they wish. I'm rarely sure who has done so, or what impact it has had. I only deeply believe that for some children it makes an essential difference for the rest of their life. It did for me. And I rest easier knowing that those children are in Christ's hands after the brief moment they were in mine.

THE NATURE OF GOD

1. The Shell

Theme: To hear God, we have to be quiet and listen.

People commonly complain that if God talks, they surely can't hear him. The Bible says that God often speaks in a whisper. Some things can only be heard if you are quiet and listen intently. If you do, you may hear some wonderful sounds. This is also true of hearing God speak to you. God can speak in a soft whisper which can only be heard in quiet meditation.

Scripture: 1 Kings 19:11–12

Device: A fairly large seashell

Goals: To teach children how to listen to God
　　　　 To encourage patience and attention to little things

Technique: Listen to a shell and you can hear the sea. Such is the common aphorism. Children are entranced by the sound of air moving in the chambers of the shell, but to hear the sound they must be very quiet. When they are quiet they are rewarded with the airy music. This is also a method by which they may hear God. The shell attracts their attention. It also allows a clear demonstration of how they may listen for God's whisper.

Ask if they know what a whisper is. Have them demonstrate. Pretending that you are hard of hearing, make them whisper louder and louder, the point being that whispers are hard to hear. God speaks in whispers. Whisper to the children, telling them they have to be very quiet to hear what you say. Repeat to them the 1 Kings story of the still, small voice. To hear God, we must be quiet and listen very carefully, just as we do when we want to hear someone whisper.

Show the children the shell, and assure them they will hear something in it if they are very quiet. Whisper to get them interested. Then place the shell over a child's ear and keep whispering for everyone to be quiet. After everyone has been able to listen, explain that often God's voice is much like the sound in the shell, quiet and soft. To hear him we must be quiet and listen very hard.

Notes: You'll need a shell large enough so the sound can be heard without great difficulty. Several shells can be used.

The response will be tremendous. Each child will want to listen three or four times.

2. What Makes Balloons Fly?

Theme: God is invisible, but can be found in what he does.

God's invisible nature causes great difficulty for people. Some will not believe in what cannot be seen. Others think God's invisibility removes him from their experience. Many people don't know where to find him. However, God can be found and experienced in one's own life through the results of his work. We find God in what he does.

Scripture: John 3:8

Device: A few balloons

Goals: To teach children how to find God
      To support their existing belief

Technique: This sermon is based upon the invisibility of the wind, a comparison Jesus uses which is recorded by John. Balloons are objects clearly affected by this invisible force. Any like object can be used.

The message is simple. You cannot see the wind, but you know it exists, because you can see what it does. You can feel it. You can hear it. The same is true with God.

Ask if any of the children have ever seen God. Some may say yes, which you can explore. Most will say no. Ask why God can't be seen. Center a dialogue around the word "invisible." Have the children tell you of things that are invisible, choosing specifically to use the wind as an example.

Discuss with the children how they know when the wind is blowing. Have them blow on their hands. They can't see the wind but they can feel it. Blow up a balloon. They can't see the wind but they can see what it does. Release the balloon, letting it fly wildly around. (Be sure to watch the children's faces when you do this. It will brighten your day.) The balloon flew because of the invisible wind coming out of it. This is how you can find the wind, because you can see and feel what it does. God is the same. We can feel him, we can hear him, we can see what God does. God is invisible, but if we look around, we will find evidence of his presence, just like the wind. Then blow up another balloon and let it go.

Notes: This sermon works very well outdoors, where there is a lot of wind activity. Use examples of the wind's activity as well as the balloons.

The balloons add color, activity, and fun.

3. Keeping Bubbles Alive

Theme: God protects us and keeps us alive.

People repress the fragile nature of their own existence, ignoring the ease with which life can die, and the delicate balance necessary for life to grow. This repression leads to the commonly believed fallacy that we are capable of protecting and sustaining our own lives. People are blinded to God as being the only true protector and sustainer of life.

Scripture: Psalm 36:5–6

Device: Bubble-blowing mixture and wand

Goals: To help children realize the frailty of life
To recognize God's love and protection
To find greater personal security

Technique: The purpose of the bubbles is to provide a physical metaphor for the frailty of life. Anyone who has played with bubbles knows they always burst or get popped. The challenge for the children is to keep the bubbles "alive," to keep them from popping. This is impossible to do, no matter how carefully they try. The point can then be made that only God can catch a bubble in his hands and keep it alive.

For a beginning, ask the children if they have any pets. Children usually do and they enjoy talking about them. What are the names of their pets? After they have told you about their animals, ask what they do to take care of them: feed, water, let outside, walk, love them. What would happen if they stopped caring for their pets? Have any of their pets ever died? (Usually at least one will have died.) Point out how hard it is to keep a pet alive and always safe.

Blow some bubbles, explaining that bubbles are like their pets. The children will probably try to pop the bubbles. Challenge them to keep the bubbles from bursting. Challenge the children to catch the bubbles in their hands and keep them alive. It can't be done. Make clear that they cannot keep a bubble alive no matter how hard they try, just as with their pets.

Blow some bubbles, explaining that the bubbles are children. Blow another bubble and name it after one of the children in the group. Tell the rest of the children to keep "David" alive. Blow a few more. Of course "David," and "Sue," and "Alice" all die too.

End by stating plainly that they all failed to keep a bubble alive. But God can do what we cannot; he can catch a bubble in his hands and keep it alive. This is what he does for each and every one of us. He holds us in his hands and protects us.

Notes: One of the benefits of using bubbles is that it involves the children in a game with which they are familiar and which they readily play. This also means they are going to enjoy themselves and be noisy. After a few moments of their popping bubbles, you may have to assert yourself so they will pay attention. But the benefits of children enjoying themselves during a sermon far outweigh the effort needed to maintain some order.

If the children do talk about pets that have died, and you can practically be sure they will, take this seriously. The death of a pet is an important experience for a child; children feel deeply about it. Express concern and compassion, listen intently. Nothing will better communicate your love and care for them.

If you have an old bubble wand, make your own bubble mixture from water and dishwashing detergent. This will allow you to make a thicker mixture than is commercially available. You save money, and a bubble from a thick mixture leaves a residue that floats in the air for a few seconds before disappearing. This gives the children a few more seconds to experience a bubble as having died.

4. The Invisible Man

Theme: God is invisible, and it is easy to ignore him.

It is easy to ignore something you can't see. The proverb "Out of sight, out of mind" has its point. God is perhaps its greatest victim. This sermon is a small play, with one of the characters an invisible man. God's invisibility causes us to treat him with little appreciation, as if he doesn't exist.

Scripture: John 1:18

Device: An empty chair

Goals: To teach respect for God
To make clear that God wants us to love him
To help the children experience what it's like to be invisible

Technique: Make the play as believable as possible. This invisible man is going to make the points in your message. Give him a name. Tell the children you want to introduce them to a special friend this morning; he's waiting behind the door. Tell them his name and ask them to be friendly. Then bring over a chair for your friend to sit in.

You're going to be an actor in this lesson. Open the door and invite him in, acting as if you can see him. After you have ushered the man into his seat, thank him for coming. Throughout the sermon you will be pretending that you are in a conversation with the invisible man, relating his words to the children.

You can converse about whatever you wish. Explain that you invited him here to tell the children what it's like to be invisible. Let him say how lonely he gets, that people treat him as if he doesn't exist. Very few people bother to say hello. They're always stepping on his toes. It's difficult to get dates, let alone go dancing. Sometimes he gets the feeling that nobody likes him or wants him around.

Throughout all this the children will be intrigued. They'll be a bit skeptical but they'll also believe somewhat. One boy kept touching the chair, running his hand over it, then proclaiming that nobody was there. But he would do it again just to make sure.

You can ask the children if they have any questions for the invisible man. Be prepared to think fast! Finally, point out for the children that God also is invisible. God also gets treated this way. God gets ignored. People don't say hello, don't talk to him. They act as though they don't care if he exists. It's easy to mistreat invisible people, but they have feelings too. We shouldn't treat anyone like that, God included. Then escort the invisible man out the door, say good-by, and close the door behind him. Leave the chair until the children leave.

Notes: Give the invisible man a distinctive name. I named him Omar. One little boy I saw at home showed me a stone with a face on it. He had named the stone Omar after that sermon.

5. Surrounded by Love

Theme: God protects us from all danger.

Trusting God to protect us is one of the hardest and most personal aspects of faith. The Bible proclaims that God will keep us safe in all things, urging us to put our trust in his power and care. But that act of trust is often more easily talked about than demonstrated. Trusting in God, though we be surrounded by danger we can still feel safe and not be harmed. We may be assured of our ultimate victory, because God is with us and around us, through all things.

Scripture: Psalm 27:1

Device: A small pail of water, a plastic sandwich bag

Goals: To teach God's promise to protect those who trust him

To encourage children to trust God

To help them experience what this protection is like

Technique: The props are meant to provide a simple, straightforward experience of being protected. The children can stick a hand into the pail and their hand will get wet. But if they place their hand in the plastic bag first, then put it in the water, it will stay completely dry. In like manner, they can be completely surrounded by danger but not harmed, because God covers and protects them.

A good introduction is to discuss their fear of the dark. Share with them your own experiences of this fear. What do they do to protect themselves in a dark room where they are scared?

Talk about how God protects everyone. They need not be afraid, because God is with them all the time in that dark room. Even when they can't see him, he is there beside them. Demonstrate with the pail of water, first without the plastic bag, then with it. God protects us like that. Danger cannot harm us, because God is around us keeping us safe.

Notes: Sharing your fears of the dark helps to legitimate their own fears and helps them feel acceptable. This tells the children that it is all right to be afraid—important support for their natural feelings, and important support for their feelings of self-worth. In sharing a fear, each person comes closer to the other in friendship.

You'll want to keep control of things with this sermon. A pail of water could become messy if some of the children become too playful.

You may also be surprised by the wonder that children express when putting their hand in water in a plastic bag. Such a simple experience is intriguing for them, though adults take it for granted.

The idea for the sermon came from dealing with my own daughter's fear of the dark. When I told her she didn't need to be so afraid, because Jesus was with her in the room, it proved immediately helpful.

6. The Flashlight

Theme: God gives us life by living in us.

The Bible makes clear that God works through people, rather than merely upon them. The New Testament has many references to Christ being "in" his believers. Having the power of God in Christ within us preserves our lives and saves us from death. God's is the power that turns our lives on to begin with; his is also the power that keeps our lives from being turned out. His power is the source of joy and security. It is important to have God working in us and through us.

Scripture: Romans 8:10–11

Device: A flashlight with batteries that can be removed

Goals: To demonstrate how God works in us
To make clear the importance of having God in us
To support a person's relationship with God

Technique: The burden of the sermon falls upon the flashlight and its battery. They will demonstrate what is otherwise an abstract idea. The flashlight works when the battery is inside and connected. When the battery is detached or removed, the flashlight does not work. This is true for ourselves too. God is like our battery: with him we light up and live. Without him we'll soon run out of power, die and stay that way.

It is important to draw a connection between the manner in which the flashlight works and the way we work. We both are dependent upon something inside.

Ask the children if there is anything they cannot do for themselves. Be sure to have some suggestions. Do they ever ask for help? It is important to find help for what we can't do alone. Ask who made us alive? God, of course. Affirm their correct answer. God makes us alive and keeps us alive; no one else can do that. We need God to stay alive, to keep from dying. We need God to be inside us, just as a flashlight needs a battery inside it.

Let the flashlight do the rest of the work. Turn it on and off. See if the children know what makes the light come on. Some undoubtedly will. To make your point, take the batteries out and let the children see that the flashlight no longer works. God is like those batteries. Unless he lives inside each one of us, our light will go out too. It is very important that the flashlight have batteries that work. Jesus came to help us understand God's love for us. When Jesus is with us, that means God is with us. God's Spirit keeps us alive and helps us do what is hard for us.

Notes: You can let the children experiment with the flashlight, turning it on and off after you've taken out the batteries, or with them still inside. It keeps the children more involved and makes the sermon more believable for them.

7. Mamas and Kitties

Theme: God loves us and cares for us.

God loves us in very real ways. Though we often refer to God as our Father, he also loves us with a mother's care. He nurtures, feeds, holds, and cuddles. God accepts, protects, and forgives. We can see the love God has for us, and offers to us, when we see love expressed between a mother and her child. God loves us in a deeply motherly way.

Scripture: Psalm 121

Device: A mother cat and her kittens

Goals: To teach how God loves us
To teach the motherly aspect of God
To help children feel loved

Technique: For this sermon idea you must have access to a cat, or some other pet, that has babies. The babies must be old enough to withstand a little touching, and the mother must be mild-mannered enough to remain calm in the midst of many children. If you have these, you can offer a wonderful example of God's love.

After reading the Scripture and explaining how those verses describe God's love, have the children gather around the box containing the mother and her kittens. The children will be enchanted, and you will have to use persistence and patience to communicate. When they have had a few moments to see the kittens, and touch them, ask what the mother cat does for her babies. Stick with it and you'll start receiving answers. When the children have listed a number of things, tell them God loves us all in exactly the same way. God loves us like a mother loves us. He feeds us, and protects us, and cleanses us, and punishes us when we need it. Be sure to make clear to the children, as they watch the cat and kittens, that they are also seeing the way God loves us all. God is like the mother cat, and we are like the kittens.

Notes: The children will become excited. You will have to maintain order to make yourself heard. Be sure all the children get a chance to see and touch the kittens. But also be firm about no one holding the babies. Once one child holds them, all the children will want to do so, and you will have no time to communicate your message. Nor will you have their interest.

8. The Story of Broken Dolls

Theme: God loves us so much he uses Jesus to make us perfect.

The center of Christianity is the atonement; it forms the saving principle of our faith. But the atonement also reveals the love of God in sacrificing his own Son, his most perfect creation.

Scripture: 1 John 4:10

Device: A story

Goals: To teach about God's love
To reveal God's great sacrifice

Technique: Read the paragraphs about storytelling in the section "Technique." Tell the following story with feeling, involving the children. Don't worry too much about morals; if the story is communicated effectively, a moral will be distilled. Read the Scripture, emphasizing God's love for us.

The Story:

God is like the man in this story who carved dolls from wood. This old man had a store in which he worked, and kept all his dolls. Sometimes he sold them; but he liked the dolls so much he didn't want to part with any of them. One night after he had gone home to bed, some robbers broke into his store, looking for money. They searched everywhere, turning over tables and breaking windows. Finally, before they left, being very mean, they broke all the dolls the old man had carved. When he returned to his store the next morning, he found the mess of broken dolls all over the floor. He was very sad. His heart was broken and he didn't know what to do. But slowly he began to pick up the pieces. He found one doll that didn't have a leg, another doll that didn't have an arm, another that didn't have a head. Since the dolls were all broken, the old man was afraid he would have to throw them out. As he continued searching through the mess, the old man remembered a doll that had not been broken. It was a very special doll, the best doll he had ever made. He kept it apart in a place where it was always very safe. He got the doll from where it was hidden. It was still in perfect condition, just as he had first made it. The old man began to think. He had the one perfect doll, but if he used the parts of that one perfect doll, he could put the rest of the dolls back together. The old man loved all his dolls so much he decided to give up the one perfect doll he had left so that the other ones could be made whole. He took a leg from the perfect doll and put it on the doll that needed a leg. He took an arm from the perfect doll and put it on the doll that needed an arm. He used the perfect doll's head and completed another doll. Finally, he used up all the parts of the one perfect doll and put all the other dolls back together. And that, in one sense, is what God and his Son Jesus did.

Notes: Embellish the story as you wish to make it more personal and effective.

THE NATURE OF JESUS

9. The Jesus Puppet

Theme: Jesus was a person in whom God's Spirit lived and worked.

It is impossible to explain completely the mystery of the nature of Jesus. Any attempt to define exactly who Jesus is must acknowledge the limits of our understanding. It is just as wrong to say that he is God as to say that he is solely man. He is both. In Philippians, Paul describes the two complementary natures of Jesus Christ, which this sermon portrays through the nature of a puppet. The outward puppet is empowered, controlled, and animated by the life behind the hand inside it. Perhaps in simple definitions we come closer to the truth than we often realize.

Scripture: Philippians 2:6–7

Device: A hand puppet

Goals: To demonstrate the nature of Jesus
To teach his likeness to us
To make Jesus tangible

Technique: This sermon rests upon the puppet metaphor. The puppet will explain by its demonstration what words could express only abstractly.

Start the children thinking about Jesus. Ask them to tell some of the wonderful things Jesus did. After they have listed some of his wonders, ask them how Jesus was able to do these things.

Tell the children that if they want to know what Jesus is like, they need only think of a puppet. Display your hand puppet. It should be big enough to cover your hand, and friendly-looking. Explain that Jesus was a person, just like each of us. He was once a little boy; he grew up and became a man. But Jesus was more than a person; Jesus was also God. Jesus was a person and God at the same time. He was like this puppet.

Play with the puppet. Tell the children the puppet is two things at the same time also. Ask them if they know what two things. A puppet is the outer face, but also it is the hand inside. Show them. The hand makes the puppet move. But the puppet face hides the hand. Can a puppet move all by itself? No, it needs the hand. Does the hand look like a person without the puppet face? No, it just looks like a hand. Jesus is like this. Inside Jesus is God's hand. But Jesus makes God's hand look like a person. When Jesus moves and does things, it is because God moves him to do so.

Notes: You will want a puppet that is friendly and warm-looking. Also one that comes off and goes on easily.

EVIL

10. What Is Evil?

Theme: Look out, because evil will cause you harm.

Evil is often regarded lightly today, sometimes being treated as a mischievous power. As this proverb says, however, evil does not bring us good; it brings disaster. It is an immense power seeking to destroy us. The Bible teaches us about sin and wrong actions so we can avoid the harm that evil will bring. We need to beware of evil, be alert, and stay away from evil for our own good.

Scripture: Proverbs 17:20

Device: A sharp knife, a piece of broken glass, a razor blade, or other dangerous items

Goals: To describe the nature of evil
To communicate the danger of evil
To teach children to stay away from evil

Technique: The props in this lesson are intended to communicate clearly, without words, a message of harm and danger. Anything that does this can be used. Knives, broken glass, and razor blades can be used with advantage because most children will have already been taught to avoid them.

Ask the children if they have heard the word "evil." What do they think it means? Ask them for examples of evil things or evil actions. What sort of person is evil? Is evil good or bad?

Explain to the children that the Bible says that anything

evil is dangerous. Do they know why? Evil can cause us great harm and great problems. It can get us in great trouble. Use the children's examples to illustrate. The Bible says we should stay away from evil things and evil persons so we won't get hurt.

Show them the props one by one, explaining how dangerous each one is. This is what evil is like. It can hurt us badly. It can kill us. It can kill others. We must be careful when we are around evil people and evil things so that we are not harmed. As much as possible, we must stay away from them.

Notes: Keep these props away from the children, in a safe place, storing them in a box when you are not using them.

11. Bad People

Theme: If someone is bad or is hurting you, the best thing to do is stay away from that person.

Learning how to handle people who hurt others or commit harmful sins is difficult, especially in a Christian framework. While we do not want to be judgmental, or separate ourselves from sinners in a way Jesus condemned, it is also not wise for us to open ourselves to needless exploitation or overwhelming temptation. Avoiding hurtful people will save us from much pain and revenge-seeking. This is especially a problem for children, who are vulnerable, easily led, and spiritually immature. It is best to stay away from those who are mean and who harm others, until our spiritual strength and personal integrity allow us to love them more actively.

Scripture: Proverbs 4:14–15

Device: A bowl filled with salt water, some pepper, liquid detergent

Goals: To teach children to stay away from people who cause harm

To support not seeking revenge

Technique: The device will illustrate the behavior you are recommending to children. Fill a bowl with salt water. Sprinkle pepper on top of the water. The pepper will float. If a small amount of liquid detergent is added to the water —on your finger, for example—the pepper will immediately rush to the sides of the bowl, away from your finger. An invisible film of detergent makes this happen, to the delight of the children.

Talk to the children of evil persons they may know about.

Are there people who would harm them? Are there bullies in school? Relate your own experience with a bully, if you have had one. What do the children do when they meet someone who means to harm them?

The Bible tells us to stay away from people who hurt others. That way they can't hurt us and we won't become like them. The Bible says if they come near, just leave them alone and go away. Don't hurt them, but also don't hang around them.

Use your demonstration to illustrate. Sprinkle the pepper on the water, explaining that the pepper represents children. Let the children decide when there is enough pepper floating on the salt water. Ask what the Bible says to do when they encounter evil persons. The Bible says to stay away from them. Place a small amount of detergent on your finger and dip it into the water. The pepper will scurry away from the bowl's center to its rim. This is what we are to do also. Stay away from evil people.

Notes: This illustration can be done only once, so make sure all the children can see.

12. Bad Things

Theme: Stay away from things that cause you trouble.

The Bible advises us to avoid evil. It is foolish, says Proverbs 27:12, to hurt yourself by walking into trouble. Unfortunately, this is something we often do. A bad habit, such as smoking, is a perfect example, which the church needs to confront. Ecclesiasticus 21:27 is too true: "When an ungodly man curses his adversary, he curses his own soul."

Scripture: Proverbs 27:12

Device: A Mr. Yucch sticker or other label that designates poison

Goals: To teach children to avoid what is bad for them, in general and specifically
To teach children to avoid smoking cigarettes

Technique: Mr. Yucch stickers are labels distributed by poison treatment centers for labeling poisonous substances. The sticker is a picture of a sick person's face, colored a noxious green, meant to communicate without words the harmfulness of a substance. It's a new style of skull and crossbones. Any label like it will work for the lesson.

When you read the proverb, read it in your own vernacular so it communicates clearly. Ask the children whether they ever get into trouble. What gets them into trouble? What happens? Help them see how they pay for their trouble and regret it later. Ask them to name some bad things adults do. I ask this so the focus is not always upon the bad things children do.

Choose a particular bad habit or practice to emphasize.

I chose smoking, placing a Mr. Yucch sticker on a pack of cigarettes. Cigarettes are poison and will make us sick if we use them. Show the pack with the sticker on it. Cigarettes can kill people. Although some of the preceding discussion may have been humorous, treat this subject seriously. Since cigarettes are poisonous and can make one very sick, the smart thing to do is to stay away from them. It is foolish to use them.

Notes: When asking for bad things that adults do, children may start discussing their parents. Depending upon the situation and on what they say, this may lead to some important sharing. But pay attention to the appropriateness of what they are saying, especially in worship; you may have to limit their response.

Other bad habits or practices you could choose to emphasize are drinking alcohol, taking drugs, careless use of weapons.

THE ATONEMENT

13. The Yardstick

Theme: Jesus took the punishment we should have received.

One of the most fundamental Christian doctrines is that of the atonement for our sins by Jesus Christ. The atonement contains two elements; this sermon deals with one. Jesus was punished in our place, for the sins we commit. Christ's atonement allows us to escape God's punishment and receive salvation. The sentence for all sinners is death. However, Jesus died for us. An understanding of this is important if we would learn about forgiveness and salvation; it is also important for revealing the tremendous love God showed in Jesus Christ. Christ suffered for us willingly, lovingly.

Scripture: Isaiah 53:4

Device: A yardstick

Goals: To teach the meaning of atonement

To reveal the love Jesus has for us

To help the children experience the meaning of God's judgment on our sin

To help them experience what it means to be saved by Jesus

Technique: A yardstick is an amazing symbol. Hold it in your hands and children get a message. Punishment. The strong symbolism of a yardstick is what makes this sermon work so well. Children immediately know what you are talking about, and the yardstick brings with it feelings that children associate with punishment.

Explain to the children that the verse in Isaiah was talking about Jesus. It tells us what Jesus did for us. Briefly state how the verse applies to Jesus. After this is done, pull out the yardstick. Smack it against the palm of your hand, or noisily against a table. Look at the children with a disciplinary glint in your eye. You'll get a response. Ask what this brings to their minds.

Have the children talk about the times they have been punished. It can become a rather humorous conversation, especially as the parents listen and react. After the children have had time to talk, ask if their brothers or sisters are ever punished. Children love to talk about this too. Ask if they ever took the place of a brother or sister who was about to be spanked. No child would likely do such a thing. Ask if they would like to have somebody take their place when they are about to get spanked. Of course they would.

This is what Jesus did. He was punished in our place. Ask the children how many of them do wrong things. All do. State that God's punishment is for anyone who does wrong. Although we were the guilty ones, Jesus took the punishment for us. He saved us. Jesus never did anything wrong, but he let God punish him instead of us. He took our place.

Notes: This sermon provides a good opportunity to include parents in the dialogue.

14. My Goodness

Theme: Because Jesus was good, all his followers are made good too.

One element of the atonement is the sacrifice that Jesus gave to satisfy the law for our sins. The second element is the righteousness accounted to us by God, as followers of Jesus Christ. Jesus was sinless, a state none of us can claim. But God treats the followers of Christ as if they too were sinless. They are regarded and rewarded as Christ himself, receiving the honor that only Jesus actually deserves. This is the second, complementary, half of the atonement. We are not only forgiven, we are rewarded and treated by God as if good, all thanks to Jesus Christ.

Scripture: Isaiah 53:5

Device: A packet of gummed gold stars, a chair

Goals: To teach the meaning of atonement
To teach how we can be made good
To help children appreciate gifts we receive from Jesus
To encourage the practice of forgiveness

Technique: A sign of good work often used in the children's classes in school is a gold star at the top of the paper. This symbol also serves the purposes of this lesson. It will help designate each child as a good person.

Begin by helping the children to admit their lack of perfection. You could ask if any of them are perfect. Or, more simply, ask if any of them are ever bad. Some may not consider themselves as being bad. If so, let them think they are not. Too soon they will reach another conclusion about themselves. Many will know they do bad things. This sermon is for those children. Get specific about the bad things they do. Ask them if they would like to be treated as good and not punished, if they only had a friend who was always good. They like that.

Pick a child who is willing to sit in the chair placed in front of the children. Explain that the person in the chair never does anything wrong. Using the children's list of specific misbehaviors, make it clear that the person in the chair never does any of those things. The person is so good that God gave the child a gold star. Put a gold star on the forehead of the child in the chair.

Then state that those who are a friend of the child in the chair can be treated as though they never do anything wrong either. All they need to do is raise their hands and ask, and they can have a gold star on their foreheads. Ask who wants one. As you give them out, be sure to ask if they are friends with the person in the chair. As long as they have the stars, they will be treated like good boys and girls, even though they do misbehave now and then. This is what Jesus does for us. He was always good. He makes each friend of his good, you and me, even though we still do wrong.

15. The Sin Eraser

Theme: Because of Jesus, God will erase our sins.

Jesus takes away our sins by taking our punishment upon himself. Our sins are erased from God's judgment. We do nothing to earn such a gift other than confess our sins to God and ask for his pardon.

Scripture: 1 Peter 2:24

Device: A chalkboard, a piece of chalk, an eraser

Goals: To teach how forgiveness is received
To offer opportunity to receive forgiveness

Technique: Set up a chalkboard in front of the children. Ask the children to tell you some of the bad things they do, some of the sins they commit. List them on the chalkboard. You can explain that God keeps track of our sins; he writes them down. If some of the children are not saying anything, ask them specifically if they ever do wrong things. Give them some ideas. Try to involve everyone, and have a sin from everyone present written on the board.

After you have a good (or bad) list, comment upon what you see. We are all capable of doing quite a few things we shouldn't; no one is perfect. Ask the children what happens if they are caught. Help them see the relationship between doing wrong and being punished.

At this point state that it is all different for Christians. We do all these wrong things, but if we confess them, God will forgive us. If we make friends with Jesus and try to do what he says, Jesus is willing to be punished in our place. Jesus will be our sin eraser. Demonstrate with your own eraser. Because of Jesus all the sins will be erased away. He can make us as if we had never done anything wrong. That is what Jesus does for those who really want to be cleansed.

Offer the children an opportunity to ask for this. Explain to them that they can ask Jesus to erase their sins and forgive them right now. They need to tell Jesus they have done wrong and to ask Jesus to be their friend. After making clear what they can say, and encouraging them, have a moment of silent prayer.

Notes: The prayer is important. So is the explanation of what the children can pray for. Pay attention to both.

16. Jesus Says

Theme: Jesus tells us to do what he says.

Jesus asks us to do what he teaches and commands. This is the mark of a true friend and disciple of Christ. In simple form, what Jesus says, his followers do. This obedience is not always easy, especially when we are not listening, or are commanded to do something we dislike. To grow in obedience to Christ we need to be aware of how we disobey and don't listen as well as commit ourselves to listen and respond.

Scripture: John 15:14

Device: A game of Simon Says

Goals: To teach the children the meaning of obedience to Jesus

To help children experience the meaning of obedience and disobedience.

Technique: Almost every child will have played the game Simon Says. This game is based upon obedience to a leader. When the leader says do something, the rest of the players respond, following the leader's example. But they can follow only if "Simon says." If the leader does something without giving verbal permission from Simon, and a player follows without that permission, the player is out of the game. The leader may say, "Simon says clap your hands." The rest of the players would be obligated to clap their hands. However, if the leader said only, "Clap your hands," anyone who did would be eliminated, because permission had not been given.

Instead of playing Simon Says, play Jesus Says. Begin with the words, "Jesus says stand up." All the children will stand up. "Jesus says jump up and down." All will jump up and down. "Jesus says yell as loud as you can." All will let out a loud roar. After a number of commands, say, "Jesus says to kiss one another." The reaction is fantastic. The children stop dead as stone and look sick. Conclude by saying, "You can sit down." They probably will sit down; but again they will have broken the rules. Jesus didn't say they could sit down. Have them all get back up, then say, "Jesus says sit down."

You can point out that they disobeyed Jesus when they weren't really listening. Jesus asks us always to do what he says, whether we like it or not. And he asks us to listen to what he says. Jesus says that if we do what he says, then we will always be his friend. Do what Jesus says.

Notes: If children can have fun in church, during worship especially, think of the benefits beyond any message they may learn. Pleasant associations give feelings which will last, and communicate on a deeper level than we often realize.

17. Yukky Water

Theme: The things we say reveal what we are like inside.

One way of gaining insight into ourselves is by observing what we say. Our statements often reflect the type of person we are. We often like to pretend that the things we say are merely externals, somehow disconnected from our self. We don't like to "own" what comes out of our mouth. But Jesus says we must. The things we say belong to us and come from inside us. Paying attention to this may provide a stimulus to change and clean up our act.

Scripture: Matthew 15:18–19

Device: Two glass pitchers and two glasses

Goals: To demonstrate the meaning of Jesus' teaching
To give children insight into themselves
To encourage the use of constructive language

Technique: Fill one pitcher with colored, muddy water. Make it look as yukky as possible. You want it to be ugly enough to make the children sure they'd get sick if they drank even a little. Fill the other pitcher with clean, clear water.

Lead the children in a discussion about bad language. Ask them if anyone has ever called them names, or made fun of them, or teased them. Do they know anyone who swears? (They'll talk more freely about someone else than about themselves.) Find out if they think this is bad behavior, and why. It is bad because it hurts people. When people hurt others it is usually because they feel mean and unhappy inside.

Show them the pitcher with the dirty water, pour a glassful, and ask who wants a drink. No one should. Ask why they don't want a drink. It's because the water is too dirty, of course; it's yukky. When people call others names, make fun of them, tease them, or swear at them, it is like spewing out dirty water. When anyone talks in a foul way it is because that person has ugly feelings inside. Make the point more personal this time, "When *you* talk badly and make fun of others . . ."

Pour a glassful from the pitcher of clean water. Ask the children if they would drink that water. When we're good inside, what comes out of our mouth is good too. When we're clean inside, we talk clean. We're good to people.

Notes: You may want to emphasize the word "yukky." It's a word with a lot of feeling in it.

Try not to emphasize swear words as much as talking badly about other people to other people, and using God's name wrongly.

18. Living Lamps

Theme: If we don't practice our faith, it will die out.

Faith without works is dead, says The Letter of James. Faith without works dies of stagnation, suffocation, and uselessness. This is what happens to those who hide their lights under bowls. Their faith dies. Oil lamps need oxygen to burn. A lamp under a bowl not only can't be seen, it dies out, as does faith without works.

Scripture: Matthew 5:15

Device: An ashtray, candlewicks, olive oil, matches, an opaque bowl

Goals: To demonstrate the importance of living as Christians
To demonstrate how lamps worked in Jesus' time
To encourage believers to live as Christians.

Technique: First, make a crude oil lamp, similar to the ones used in the time of Jesus. They were often simple, plain devices (though not always) which looked like a combination of an ashtray and a three-cornered hat. The wicks were laid in the grooves and burned the oil which they soaked out of the inner basin. Modern-day ashtrays work perfectly for this. Select one that has two to four grooves for holding cigarettes, and is round.

Fill the inside with olive oil, lay pieces of candlewick in the grooves, allowing the wicks to soak up the oil. Then light the wicks. A smoky, low-grade light is produced, much like the light from the lamps in ancient times. Explain to the children what a lamp was like in Jesus' day and how it worked.

Much of this sermon keys upon the meaning of faith. The children need an idea of what dies if we don't obey Jesus. Using the lamp, tell them that if we follow and obey Jesus, he gives us faith. (Faith is a gift of the Spirit.) And faith is like a lamp. Light the lamp and let them see how it gives us light so that we can see in the dark. It keeps us warm if we're cold. It helps to protect us. This is what Jesus gives us; everyone who follows him has one of these little flames inside.

Jesus says it is foolish to have a lamp and hide it. When you hide the lamp you can't see it or feel it; it can't keep you safe or protected. Not only that, it goes out. Demonstrate by putting a bowl over the burning lamp. Ask the children what they think happens. Point out to them that they can't see the lamp anymore. Then pick up the bowl after a while and, *voilà,* a dead lamp! This is what happens if we don't obey Jesus and do what he tells us. Our faith, our inner lamp, dies out.

Notes: You will need to know how much time it takes for your lamp to extinguish itself under the bowl. This will give you an idea of how long to wait during the lesson before revealing the dead lamp to the children.

19. Jesus Seeds

Theme: Christians grow up to become like Jesus Christ.

Large fruits can come from small seeds; small beginnings can have large endings. Paul says we are called to grow into "the very height of Christ's full stature" (Ephesians 4:13), from the seed first planted in us by the hearing of God's Word. Jesus himself uses the analogy of the Christian message being like a seed, planted in us and growing until we are all like him. That seed has been planted in all who are Christians.

Scripture: Luke 13:18–19

Device: Any large vegetable and its seed, such as a Hubbard squash

Goals: To demonstrate Jesus' parable
To increase the children's belief in the possibility of their own spiritual growth

Technique: The purpose of the vegetable and its seed is not simply to display the props Jesus used; it is to show, tangibly, how a large fruit can come from a small seed. This seemingly obvious truth is difficult for Christians to believe about themselves. They cannot believe that the small seed planted in them could ever produce a Christlikeness, especially in such poor soil. But it can and will.

Show the children the seeds. Ask them what it is you have in your hands, and where they have seen these things before. Let them guess what your seeds might grow into. When they have taken some guesses, display the large Hubbard squash which the seeds produced. Help the children experience its size. Let them try to hold it or pick it up. Make it clear that the little seeds you have in your hands will become a large squash like the one they are trying to lift.

Explain that little seeds can grow into big things. Inside each child a little seed of faith was planted when the child started coming to church. Let the children see the seeds, so they can visualize what you are talking about. Each time they come to church the seed is watered and fed. Someday it will grow up and make each of them more like Jesus. Those seeds are growing right now. And just as those small seeds made that big squash, so the little Jesus seeds will one day make them like Jesus.

Give each child a squash seed. Tell the children to remember that faith is growing inside them. This little seed is to help them expect that their faith will continue to grow.

Notes: Any large vegetable will do. Instead of a Hubbard squash, a pumpkin or a watermelon can be used.

Hide the vegetable and reveal it after the children have guessed what the seeds might produce. The children are duly impressed with how large a fruit can come from such a small seed.

20. The Friend

Theme: Friendship is proven by acts of kindness.

Jesus instructs us to be friends to all people. But, as Jesus teaches, friendship means much more than saying that someone is our friend. Friendship involves acts of kindness, sacrifice, and compassion for others. Without actions, friendship is meaningless.

Scripture: Luke 10:30–37

Device: A story

Goals: To teach the meaning of love and friendship
To encourage acts of true friendship

Technique: Refer to the paragraphs on storytelling in the section "Technique." The following story takes one of the parables of Jesus and reworks it into the idiom and situations of today. The use of a Samaritan as the hero of the story was a radical choice. Samaritans were considered outcasts and heretics by the orthodox Jewish people. Yet it is a Samaritan who helps the person in need, while the self-righteous religious people walk on by.

Read the parable for yourself, but do not read it aloud to the children. We are seeking to rework Jesus' story, not create a new one. Fill in the story's roles with characters viable for your community. Who are the outcasts who could be the compassionate Samaritan? Who are the self-righteous elite who walk by on the other side of the road? Change the characters and details to revitalize the meaning of the parable.

The Story:

There once was a man who was hitchhiking from_____
_____to_____. While he was on his way, a
car came too close and struck him. He was knocked into the
ditch beside the road, and he lay there unconscious. The
people in the car stopped; but seeing him, they thought he
was dead and quickly drove away. It wasn't long after this
had happened that a car driven by a minister came along.
The minister saw the man and slowed down; however, he
was to speak to the Rotary Club and could just make it if
he pressed on. Anyway, he thought, an ambulance was probably on the way. After the minister had gone by, another car
came down the road driven by an officer of the church. It
was payday, and the church member was headed into_____
_____to deposit money in the bank and buy groceries.
She saw the man lying in the ditch, but thought he was just
a drunk who had passed out. She didn't dare stop to help
him. So she drove on. Finally, a_____man in an
old car came down the road, saw the injured man lying
there, and felt sorry for him. He stopped his car and went
over to the man. Wiping the dirt off the injured man's face,
the_____man picked him up, put him in the car,
and drove to the hospital. After the injured hitchhiker had
been taken to the emergency room, the_____man
went to the business office of the hospital and said he would
pay all the costs for the man who was hurt.

"Which one of these three people acted like a friend
toward the hitchhiker who had been hit by a car?" Let the
children respond. When they have given the correct answer,
tell the children they are right, and Jesus says to go and do
the same.

Notes: Now this parable will be heard by everyone.

21. Salt

Theme: Christians, like salt, change what they touch.

Few sayings of Jesus are more easily understood from daily experiences. We are all familiar with salt and its effect upon food. A little bit of salt can change and enhance a food's taste; salt can preserve food and purify it. This is what Christians are called to do in the world. Christians are to purify, enhance, and preserve the world. They are to change it.

Scripture: Matthew 5:13

Device: A saltshaker, two glasses of water

Goals: To experience the meaning of this teaching
To challenge the children to do what Jesus says

Technique: All the children will be familiar with salt and saltshakers. They use them all the time at home. However, the children probably have never drawn the connection between Christians and salt. This lesson provides an opportunity for them to see and taste what Jesus meant.

Hold up a saltshaker and have the children identify it. Center a short discussion upon salt and its uses. Salt changes the taste of food. Jesus says that Christians are to be like salt. Beforehand, pour two glasses of water, mixing a quantity of salt with the water in one glass. After you have discussed salt, and the comparison that Jesus makes, have the children study the two glasses of water. Tell them one glass contains plain water and the other salt water. See whether they can distinguish them by sight. Have them taste the water, offering a sip to each child who wants one. See whether they can tell the difference. The children will be able to tell without question. Have them sip from both glasses so they can notice the change that salt makes.

Explain that this is what salt does. It changes things. This is what Christians do too. Instead of changing food, we change people and the world around us. We make this world a nicer place in which to live. Have the children list things they can do to make the world a better place. Then challenge them to do it.

Notes: The list of changes they can make will depend upon how much time you have and the ages of the children. It is most effective if some form of follow-up is possible. Discuss at the next meeting whether the children did what they said they would. Were they able to change something for the better? Have some ideas ready of what the children could do.

Don't let the glass of water out of your hands when the children sip from it. If you do, both the lesson and the glass will be out of your control.

22. Sugar and Salt

Theme: You can only tell Christians by the results they have.

It is difficult to tell who is truly a Christian. So many people can look like Christians, can appear to be living the life to which we are called. But, as Jesus indicated when he talked about wolves in sheep's clothing, appearances can be deceiving. Not everyone who looks like a Christian is one. Not everyone who appears to be living a Christian life is having a Christlike effect upon those around him or her. This difference is important because it helps us to judge ourselves. The question is not what we look like, it is what effect we are having upon the world.

Scripture: Matthew 5:13

Device: Two saltshakers, one filled with salt, the other with sugar; two bowls or cups

Goals: To teach the meaning of discernment
To give criteria for evaluating Christians
To challenge us to be active Christians

Technique: This lesson is based upon the difficulty of telling sugar and salt apart. The easiest way to distinguish salt from sugar is by the taste. We determine their identity from their results, because their appearance confuses us.

Pour some salt into one of the cups and sugar into the other. Jesus says we are to be like salt. Can the children tell which one of the cups holds salt? Have them study the cups, but don't let them taste. When they have made a guess, ask if they are sure. Make clear how easily the two substances are confused. They look alike. Jesus tells us to be like salt;

but it is easy to look like salt when we are not. It is easy for a person to look like a Christian even though the person may be really something else. Ask the children what is the best way of telling the difference between sugar and salt. Have them taste each and then tell you which cup contains which. The same is true for Christians. We can't tell who is a Christian by what the person looks like. We can only tell Christians by what they do.

Notes: You can add a little twist at the beginning by filling both cups with sugar. This emphasizes more strongly the difficulty of telling salt and sugar apart. Then repeat with both sugar and salt and have the children guess again.

This lesson is a good follow-up to the one on "Salt." It points up doing as opposed to appearances. Use this follow-up to discuss whether the children did what they agreed to do concerning helping things change for the better.

23. The Important Thing

Theme: All we do in church has meaning only if we love Jesus.

After spending a number of years working in a church, I realize that people often lose touch with why they are involved. They can become so busy with groups, committees, suppers, choirs, cleaning, teaching that it seems the activities become more important than the One who provides the excuse for them, Jesus Christ. The expression of love for Jesus is easily lost in a person's work. But work in a church is service for a person you love. The truly important thing, amid all these other important items, is our love of Jesus Christ. Do you feel love for him in your heart?

Scripture: Matthew 7:22–23

Device: A picture of Jesus; a number of articles used in activities in the church

Goals: To teach an ordering of values

To teach the primary importance of Christ in our lives

To encourage and support feelings of love for Jesus

Technique: The purpose of this lesson is to bring to mind all the different work that is done in church, and then show what must be present to make it worth doing. Gather a number of articles that will remind the children of various aspects of the church's work: dish towel, Bible, Sunday school book, bus keys, hammer, broom, music sheet. Any clear symbol of church programs can be used. Have the children tell you about the various activities of the church.

Personalize the different works, relating how people are involved in each one.

After the children have listed a number of different works, tell them that one thing is more important than all of these. There is only one reason that all these activities are even done. See if they know or can guess. Hold up a picture of Jesus that they will recognize. Before we do anything in the church we must love Jesus. Loving Jesus is more important than anything else. After placing all the other props behind you, hold the picture in front and tell the children that loving Jesus must come first. Close by thanking Jesus, as demonstrated in the lesson "Giving Thanks."

If there is time, have the children discuss how they show love for someone. One way is by doing things for the person. People work in the church to demonstrate their love for Jesus. How do the children show Jesus that they love him?

Notes: You can use a cross to symbolize Jesus, but that may be too abstract for some children. A picture of Jesus, while inaccurate in a sense, is more concrete and easily understandable.

24. Generosity

Theme: Jesus wants us to give generously from what we have.

It is never too early to learn stewardship, and not just of money, but of all the things God has given us. Many children witness their parents giving to the church grudgingly, sparingly, after all other expenses and luxuries have been provided. This is not what Jesus teaches. He teaches us to give generously, dedicating all we have to God's use rather than to ourselves.

Scripture: Mark 12:41–44

Device: A piece of bubble gum for each child

Goals: To educate about unselfish giving
To experience being given to
To be rewarded for being in the church

Technique: Have enough pieces of bubble gum so you can reasonably expect to give each child a piece. The object is to have enough so that no one gets left out. Have the gum in your pocket, giving the impression that there is just enough to go around.

Explain briefly what Jesus meant by what he said in this story. The poor widow who gave only a few pennies offered more than the men who gave $100, because she gave from the money she needed to live on; the others gave from their bank accounts. Jesus teaches us to give generously, not simply to provide for ourselves.

Tell the children you have some bubble gum which you were looking forward to chewing, but you are willing to share. Ask those who would like a piece of bubble gum to raise their hands. Give gum to those children whose hands are raised, encouraging the others to take some also. Children will be shy about asking, or they may have been taught not to take from other people. However, I have yet to meet a child who dislikes bubble gum and who truly doesn't want any if it is offered. Try to leave no one out. Most likely, as you begin to hand out the gum and the children see that you are serious, they will start to raise their hands. As you hand it out, comment upon how many of them want gum, asking out loud if you have to give all of them gum. Would Jesus want you to give all of them gum? It's amazing how quickly children can answer yes. As you near the end, begin to grumble a little about having given away so much. When you are down to the last child, ask if Jesus means that you must give that child a piece too. Do we have to share and give generously? The answer is yes.

This is what Jesus teaches us: to give generously from what we have. We are to share with all people.

Notes: This is a good example of church being fun, and providing fun is as important as communicating the message. When children enjoy themselves and come away with something tangible and good, other children, reluctant to participate, may be encouraged to come.

Be sure to stress that the pieces of gum are to be taken home unwrapped and unused.

25. Strength in Bunches

Theme: As Christians, we are stronger when grouped together.

Why go to church? Why have fellowship with other Christians? These are common questions, asked by people who would otherwise quickly acknowledge there is strength in numbers. Nations are strong because their many people are banded together, sharing their talents for the protection of all. The same is true of Christians, who must live in this world. Alone we will be crushed by the nations and cultures of this non-Christian world, seduced out of our Christian values, trained out of faith. Together, supporting each other, we cannot be broken as easily. Together we will find ourselves much more able to hold our faith and values firm.

Scripture: Matthew 12:25

Device: Ten to twenty pencils, a rubber band

Goals: To demonstrate strength in numbers
To support church involvement
To foster a sense of togetherness

Technique: Every schoolboy tries his hand at breaking pencils. Holding each end between your fingers you whack the pencil on your knee, a child's version of karate. After explaining what Jesus taught—that alone we are much weaker than together—use the pencils to demonstrate his teaching.

Hold out a pencil and challenge one of the children to break it. There should be no problem in finding a volunteer. There is something satisfying in breaking a pencil. Let a few children do it. Then challenge the children to break two pencils at the same time, holding them together. Let those who wish try; some will break the pencils, but with more difficulty. Then challenge the children to break three pencils at once. They probably will not be able to accomplish this. Finally, offer a reward to any child who can break a group of ten pencils bound together by a rubber band.

The lesson is obvious. The more pencils you group together, the harder they become to break. The same is true for us as Christians. The more we band together, the stronger we are. When we group together we find it much easier to live as Christians. We live in a world where it is hard to be a Christian; that's why it is important for Christians to get together as we do in church. It makes us much stronger.

Notes: Pay attention when the children break the pencils. Don't let them hurt themselves. If the pencils don't break easily, don't let the children go whacking away.

26. Different but the Same

Theme: Though we are all different, as Christians we are all the same.

Christianity paved the way for social, racial, and sexual equality. In Christ there is no difference between persons. Though we each are different, in Christ we are the same. There is no excuse or Scriptural justification for any kind of prejudice or stereotyping.

Scripture: Galatians 3:28

Device: A new box of crayons

Goals: To demonstrate difference but sameness
To speak against prejudice
To encourage acceptance of others

Technique: The crayons in the box are different in color, but otherwise they are exactly the same. This is the sermon's metaphor. People can be different in color, or sex, or age; but, as Christians, they are all the same. We are to treat all people the same.

Lead the children in a short discussion of the differences they see between people in church. Some are elderly, some are short, some are men, some women. If there are no racial distinctions, ask the children if they have ever been around other races. Have they ever been with black people? Have they ever been with Chinese, or Indians? How do they feel with people who are different? Do they like people of the opposite sex? Do they like people who are very short? Would they like to stay overnight in a black person's house? in a Chinese family's house?

After some discussion, dump the crayons in front of the children. Ask what differences they can see between the crayons. Are they made of the same stuff? Does one crayon break just as easily as another? The crayons are different colors, but that is the only difference. This is the way it is with Christians. People may look different or have a different color, but inside they are the same. People in our church may look different in many ways. However, we are all the same. What makes us the same? We are all Christians. Since we are all Christians, there is no difference between a white person and a black person, a Chinese person and an Indian, an older person and a younger person, a girl and a boy, a dwarf and a giant. We are all the same in Christ and we are to treat everyone the same.

Notes: Adapt this to whatever prejudices are most notable in your community.

27. The Phone

Theme: Prayer is talking with God.

Prayer is as simple as a conversation, only it is conversation with the invisible God. The invisibility is what makes prayer seem complicated. But Jesus teaches, and shows us, that in our personal meditations we can communicate with the Creator. It is as if we are talking on the phone. God receives our praise, hears our needs, and responds by communicating with us. We have a direct line to God.

Scripture: Matthew 6:5–6

Device: A phone

Goals: To teach what prayer is
To teach how to pray
To support children who do pray
To encourage prayer

Technique: A phone is a clear symbol of communication, especially with someone who is not present. What child has not talked on a phone to someone far away? The child can't see the person, but the two of them can talk back and forth. This is what prayer is.

Talk to the children about prayer and their prayer life. When do they pray? What have they prayed about? To whom are they talking? Define what prayer is and describe what happens. God hears what we are saying, even when we only think it. That's why we can pray silently. Then God will answer our prayers in some way. Prayer can be used to ask God for things and to thank him.

Show the children the phone. Prayer is like talking on the phone to God. He hears what we say; he hears what we want and need. He hears what we think and knows what scares us, even though we can't see him. Talking to God is like talking on the phone. In fact, when we pray, we can pretend we are talking on the phone.

Close by praying together.

Notes: Praying with the children is worth some thought on your part beforehand. In a worship service, where there are time limitations, it may be easier to have the children all join hands in a circle and one person pray aloud, perhaps you yourself. In a small study group, it is meaningful to ask for prayer requests and give each child a chance to pray out loud. I ask the children if they want to pray aloud, encouraging them to do so, but I never insist. They are free to do as they choose. After I have asked, we then take turns. Some children always have prayed out loud, even in the worship service, and I always pray with them.

Sharing prayer requests can be an important time of closeness, when needs and problems are brought forth. Pay attention to what the children say and treat it seriously.

28. Call Him by Name

Theme: When you want help from Jesus, call on him by name.

The Scriptures contain much advice and guidance about prayer. They also contain many promises about the power of prayer. The verses selected are both a promise and a teaching. When we pray we are to do it as conscious followers of Jesus Christ. We are to mention him expressly in our prayers, stating that it is he we follow. God is the unlimited source of power to people, through Jesus Christ, God's personal manifestation. In prayer we can tap that power by praying in the name of his incarnate Son. In this we have a blessing not possible in the Old Testament. God, by becoming a person, gave us a name for our use in praying.

People will address God by many different names in prayer, using whatever name is most meaningful for them. To think of Jesus as representing God's love for us is especially helpful for children. They can understand God as a person. This is not wrong. In fact, it is one of the purposes for which God embodied himself.

Scripture: John 14:13–14

Device: A dialogue

Goals: To educate about prayer
To encourage children to pray
To support those who do pray

Technique: The practicality of having a name is obvious from daily life. Names are the primary means by which we identify ourselves. We direct our comments to other individuals by using their names. This is also done in prayer as taught by Jesus. To receive his help, direct your comments to him.

This can be made clearly understandable to children. Children learn early the significance of a name. They learn that they have a name, as do others. Names are among the first words they speak. A name is one of the things that makes each child special. Ask the children if they have a name; have them raise their hands if they do. Once they have all raised their hands, ask what their names are, even though you may already know. Give them a chance to tell you. After all the children have given their names, lead a short discussion about the importance of names. If their mother wants them to do something, she calls them by name. "Billy, come over here and pick up your toys." Her use of the name is how we can tell to whom she is speaking.

Ask the children a question: "If I wanted one of you to stand up, how would you know which of you I meant?" They'll know the answer, after the preceding discussion. You would call them by name. Demonstrate by doing exactly that. Ask one of them, by name, to stand up. Explain again why you used a name. If there aren't too many children in the group, ask each one by name to do something.

Explain that Jesus says we are to do the same in our prayers. If we want to talk to Billy, we call Billy by name; if we want to talk to Jesus, we call Jesus by name. Jesus can bring us God's help. Whenever we want that help, we call on Jesus, and he will help us. That's how Jesus knows we are talking to him. Jesus says that if we ask him for anything in his name, he will do it. So, when we want to talk with Jesus, or want help from Jesus, we call him by name. That's how he knows we are talking to him.

Notes: If time permits, lead the children in a discussion about prayer. Do they pray? How often? What do they pray for? Give support for any kind of praying they may do! Discuss the purposes for prayer. What good does it do?

One quick thinker asked me about people who have the same first name. I then showed him the importance of middle names.

29. Follow the Leader

Theme: Disciples are people who follow Jesus.

Jesus says clearly that his disciples are to do as he commands. His disciples are to follow him, obey his teachings, and imitate his actions. It is a simple concept. The difficulty lies in the doing, for Jesus leads us into difficult and dangerous situations.

Scripture: Matthew 9:9

Device: A game of Follow the Leader

Goals: To demonstrate the meaning of obedient following
To help the children experience being a follower
To encourage them to be disciples

Technique: Jesus asks Matthew to follow him and Matthew does as he is asked. He gets up and follows Jesus. It sounds like a game of Follow the Leader, which fits nicely into the format of the lesson.

Follow the Leader is a simple game in which the leader leads the other children, who must do whatever the leader does. If the leader walks, they walk. If the leader runs, they run. If the leader hops, they hop. Most children know how to play; if not, they fall into it naturally.

Make sure the story about Matthew is clear to the children. What did Matthew do? Explain that they are going to be like Matthew and play a game of Follow the Leader. Ask who wants to play. Give those who don't permission to stay in their pew until you return. Then set out on an excursion around the church. Use your imagination. It can be fun to have the children tiptoe very quietly. Go in and out of rooms, weave around, run, hop, skip, turn in circles.

The possibilities are endless. Just end up back where you began.

After the game is finished, explain that being a Christian is like playing a game of Follow the Leader. Jesus is the leader. Wherever he goes, whatever he says, we do. Just as Matthew did. When we are a Christian we follow Jesus. That's all we have to do.

Notes: A child who doesn't want to play should not be pressured to conform. An unwilling participant could disrupt the effect of the game. When I faced such a situation, I played it safe and asked an adult to watch over the child while we were playing the game.

30. Parts Together

Theme: A church is many different individuals joined together.

Paul describes the church as Christ's body—many different parts, each part having a different function but all bound to one another. We all need others. We need to have a conscious recognition of our unity.

Scripture: Romans 12:4–5

Device: Forming an ever-expanding circle

Goals: To experience togetherness and separateness
To encourage reaching out to others

Technique: This lesson was originally designed as a worship experience for children and adults. It could be done in a class of children only, but it would lose some of its meaning. All the people in the church, joined together, provide an important experience.

Call the children to the front of the sanctuary. Read the Scripture and briefly explain what Paul means. Then have the children gather in a circle, holding hands with one another. When we are together we are the church. Have them unclasp their hands. We all live in different places, have different names, do different things. When we get together, holding hands, then we are the church.

Have each child go and bring someone from the congregation to the front of the church. Form a circle using the children plus the people they brought with them. Again go through the meaning of hands apart and hands held. Have every person at the front then go and bring someone else. Each time, form a circle holding and dropping hands, with everyone going out and returning with someone else. Repeat this, making ever-expanding circles, until every person in the church has been brought into the circle. Stretch the circle around the sanctuary, everybody holding hands. When the entire congregation has been made into a circle, read what Paul said in Romans 12:6–13. These are Paul's directions for all church members; it is meaningful to hear them directed to us while we are holding hands with one another. Then close the session with a hymn. If it is at the end of the service, everyone can hold hands for the benediction.

Notes: This is a worship experience everyone enjoys and benefits from. Children form the right type of beginning with their qualities of openness. They have a great deal of fun bringing people forward from the congregation. It is also a good experience to have all the people in the church, regardless of age, bound together.

31. Lifting a Weight

Theme: When Christians work together they can do what they cannot do separately.

Help carry one another's burdens. This is a command of Christ which Paul writes to the Galatians. In fact, it is the only way a burden can be carried, unless it is very small. Together we can lift much more weight than we ever could separately. The burden of living in a non-Christian world is so great, the needs so overwhelming, that Christians must band together if they are going to grow and respond effectively. When Christians do this, a church is formed. When they do not help carry the burden, they are not truly a church.

Scripture: Galatians 6:2

Device: A barbell

Goals: To demonstrate strength in numbers
To experience burdens and personal weakness
To teach how burdens may be carried
To support those who ask for help

Technique: Add enough weight to each end of the barbell so that a child will not be able to lift it alone. That can be hard to figure out. I thought I had done it when a boy proceeded to lift the barbell from the ground. If that occurs, it is not disaster, however, for most of the children will not be able to lift the weight.

Give each child a chance to lift the weight. Let each experience how difficult, or impossible, it is to pick the barbell up. After all who wish have tried, ask all the children to try lifting the barbell together. You join in too. Together you can do it. Hold the weight in the air for a few moments so they can savor having a hand in the achievement. They enjoy it. Lower the weight back to the ground and point out what you read from Paul's letter. Christians help to carry one another's burdens. We all helped pick up that weight. When we worked together we were acting like Christians. Have the children work together with you once more. This time, when you have the weight in the air, explain that a church is where Christians get together to work and lift big burdens. The people get together to help one another.

Notes: Be extremely careful! Squashed children beneath a barbell do not add much to a worship service. Do not let the children attempt to lift the barbell together without your help. Be sure the barbell will not be dropped accidentally. Make the weight light enough so that you yourself can lift the barbell without a problem. If a child manages to lift it, watch closely to make sure the weight is put down again safely. With a little caution on your part, this can be an effective lesson.

32. Trusting Arms

Theme: Faith means trust.

A simple definition of faith is trust. It is possible to weight the meaning of faith down with so many ideas, demands, and promises that its basic dynamic is lost. When you have faith in God, you trust him. Perfect faith is to trust completely. This simple definition makes faith difficult. Jesus says this ability to trust both him and our Creator is the key to the Christian life.

Scripture: Psalm 27:14

Device: A trust game

Goals: To experience the meaning of trust
To help the children to trust you
To encourage their trust in Christ

Technique: This lesson is straight out of adult group experiences. Groups for personal growth utilize exercises that test and broaden a person's ability to trust other people. This particular exercise is simple, but it communicates the message clearly. Someone stands before you, back to you. You challenge that person to fall backward, promising that you will not allow him or her to hit the floor. The person will fall backward only if there is trust in what you have promised.

Read the verse from the psalm and lead the children in dialogue about the word "faith." How many of them have heard the word before? What do they think it means? Point out that the verse equates faith with trust. Focus upon trust as the dynamic of faith. What does trust mean? What persons do they trust? Tell them you have a demonstration.

Arrange with someone beforehand to demonstrate the exercise for the children. Explain to the children what you are going to do. Then have that person stand before you and fall backward into your arms. After the demonstration, ask the children if any of them trust you enough to fall backward into your arms, as was just done. If no one volunteers, ask someone specifically. Whether or not the children volunteer, their response can still be used to make your point. Faith means trust. The children exhibited either trust or lack of it. They know how trust feels and what it is like. When you have faith in Jesus you are willing to take him at his word. You are willing to do anything Jesus says, because you trust him. Faith means that you believe his promises, you can rely upon his guidance and help.

Notes: Any exercise that gives a person an experience in the meaning of trust will accomplish the same purpose. For example, persons may be blindfolded and then led on a walk.

THE MEANING OF CHRISTMAS

33. Blowing Kisses

Theme: God shows he loves us in the baby Jesus.

The inspiration for this lesson came from the hymn "Love Came Down at Christmas." The meaning of Christmas and the knowledge that God loves us go hand in hand. God sent his love into the world in the baby Jesus. God loves you. That is why Jesus was born, and why we celebrate Christmas today.

Scripture: Luke 2:8–12

Device: Enough chocolate kisses to give one to each child

Goals: To communicate the meaning of Christmas
To communicate a Christmas feeling of love and warmth
To help the children know that God loves them

Technique: The chocolate kisses are meant only to serve as reminders of what will be said in the lesson. Children like chocolate kisses, and good feelings are attached to them. The name "kisses" suggests love and affection. Using them is an effective way to bring back to the child's mind the ideas of love, fun, and feeling good, all at once. The important aspect of this lesson is to provide the information you want the candy to reinforce and recall.

Begin by asking the children how people show they love you. Hugs, kisses, presents: the children can talk about this for quite a while. Who gives them love? To whom do they give love? Ask if they have ever blown someone a kiss. Some will be mystified; some will know what you mean. Have those who know demonstrate blowing kisses for those who don't know. Blow some kisses back to the children. Simply state that Christmas is the time God blew a kiss to everybody on earth, to you and to me. The baby Jesus was God's kiss, and he blew the kiss down to us from way up in heaven. God wanted to show that he loves us. Then distribute the candy kisses, explaining that the candy is a reminder of what Christmas' means. Christmas is the time God blew a kiss to every one of us, because God loves us. God loves you, and you, and you.

Notes: Be sure you have a chocolate kiss for each child. Especially at Christmastime you don't want any child to be left out. If you can provide enough for the whole congregation, distribute a chocolate kiss to every person after the service, as a reminder of God's love for all people.

PALM SUNDAY

34. Giving Thanks

Theme: On Palm Sunday, people give thanks to Jesus.

Palm Sunday is the day the populace acclaimed Jesus as savior and king, not knowing all the tragedy that was soon to come. This is how we most often remember the day, as a prelude to Jesus' death and resurrection. It is a day for giving thanks to Christ, something many people rarely do.

Scripture: Mark 11:1–10

Device: Some palm branches

Goals: To communicate the meaning of Palm Sunday
To help the children experience the day's meaning
To praise Jesus

Technique: If your church distributes palm branches on Palm Sunday, then you have what you need for the lesson. If not, try to get some. Begin with a short discussion about the meaning of Palm Sunday. What were all those people doing with their palm branches? What does the word "hosanna" mean? Tell the children they are going to do what those people in Jesus' time did on Palm Sunday. They are going to have Palm Sunday right now in church. They are all going to give Jesus thanks by waving their palm branches over their heads and shouting "Thank you!" as loud as they can. Ask the children what they want to thank Jesus for. Each time they mention something, have the children wave their palms and yell "Thank you!" The list of reasons can be endless. For an especially important one, such as giving thanks to Jesus for dying for us, have them yell thank you twice. At the end, simply state that this was what Palm Sunday was like long ago. The people then were doing for Jesus what the children just did; they gave Jesus thanks.

Notes: You will have to let your inner child loose on this one. Wave your palm branch and shout the thank you's. At first the children are bound to be a little reticent, and you will have to challenge them to shout louder. Keep challenging them until their shouts are loud enough for this to be a satisfying experience for them.

This is a good chance for you to loosen up your congregation a little bit, if you think they need it, by injecting some enthusiasm and emotion.

It is a good idea to distribute palm branches on Palm Sunday. They serve as a physical reminder of the meaning of the day.

This idea can be reworked for any occasion for giving thanks. Have the children wave their hands over their heads instead of waving palms.

EASTER

35. The Candle That Won't Go Out

Theme: Easter celebrates the day that Jesus came back to life.

Easter is a combination of two things: an event and the human response to the event. The event is the resurrection —Jesus, who was dead, comes back to life. The human responses are surprise, wonder, and joy at witnessing a miracle.

Scripture: Mark 16:1–6

Device: A trick birthday candle that relights, two regular birthday candles, matches

Goals: To demonstrate the meaning of resurrection

To help the children experience the Easter surprise and wonder

Technique: What God did in the resurrection of Jesus Christ can be demonstrated by the use of a trick birthday candle. It is an amazing device which can be completely blown out and then spontaneously relights in twenty to thirty seconds. The effect is to see something seemingly dead come back to life. Except for those children who know how to recognize these trick candles, the result will be unexpected.

Ask the children what happened at Easter. Some are bound to know. Then stage a simple replay of the passion, using the trick candle. Set the three candles in a row, the trick one in the middle, to resemble a miniature Calvary. Do this ahead of time, and make sure the candles are firmly held in place. Light the middle candle and tell the story about Jesus, how he was arrested, sentenced to die, and crucified with two other persons. Light the other two candles. It was on crosses that all three men died. Blow out all three candles. While the candles are out, tell the children how sad Jesus' friends were. Fill in time talking about Jesus and his death until the candle relights. Then you can jump back in surprise, asking what happened. Who lit that candle? Who has the matches? You mean it relit all by itself? That's what Jesus did. Like that candle, Jesus came back to life. He is like a light that shines in the darkness and the darkness cannot extinguish it.

Notes: My recommendation is not to involve the children in blowing out the candles. This is based on personal experience. It is Easter, and the children are apt to be supercharged. They blew so forcefully that all my candles fell over. Also, having had my permission to blow out the candles once, when the candle in the middle relit they began to puff away again. The candle never had a chance. Tell the lesson as a story, with the children watching from a short, but respectful, distance.

This lesson also requires faith on your part that the candle will relight. Twenty or thirty seconds can seem like forever, and is ample time to have many anxiety attacks, wondering what you will do if that candle does not relight. God is more dependable than a mass-produced candle.

The children are bound to be excited on Easter. Be prepared to deal with that excitement without quashing their fun and good feelings. Work with their excitement.

THE CHURCH

36. The Web

Theme: As Christians, and members of a church, we are all connected together.

A church is a collection of connected Christians who compose a fragile unity. This unity has to be actively preserved, because it can be easily strained, broken, or rendered ineffective. The actions of one person affect the entire network of related Christians. We must always bear in mind our connectedness as a church.

Scripture: Ephesians 4:2–3

Device: A ball of yarn

Goals: To demonstrate the connectedness of Christians in a church

To experience the meaning of connectedness

Technique: Announce that you are going to demonstrate what a church is like. Have the children stand in a circle, holding out their hands. Using the yarn, tie one end of the yarn around the wrist of one child; then make a weblike pattern, wrapping the yarn around the wrists of each of the other children. End with yourself. Don't simply go around the circle, but crisscross. This makes a more direct, and more easily felt, connection.

When you are done, explain to the children that a church is like crisscrossed yarn: it is a group of Christians bound to one another by Jesus Christ. The actions of one person affect everybody else. Demonstrate by having one child start walking. What does the movement do to the other children? They are pulled by the yarn and must start walking too. Have the child stop, and ask another child to walk in another direction. Again, the children follow because they are connected to one another. This is the way a church works. If people don't follow or give in, the connections are pulled, strained, and sometimes broken. Have two or three children sit down. What does that do to the rest? The other children must sit down too, or endure pressure from the yarn. We are connected to each other in a church, and Paul says we must be careful how we act so that we do not strain the entire web. Have a child start walking and instruct the other children not to move. Then have two children start walking in different directions at the same time. What happens to the web and the yarn? We must always be careful about what we do, and how it affects the church and everyone in it.

Conclude by restating the meaning of the demonstration, and what it means for us as members of a church to be bound to one another.

Notes: Be careful when the demonstrations are taking place that no child's wrist is pinched too tightly by the yarn. Do not tie or wrap their wrists too tightly, but neither do you want too much slack in the connections.

You must be especially careful when the children are walking in opposite directions.

If everyone is careful, this demonstration can be very effective.

37. Building Blocks

Theme: A church is Christians working together.

How I wish more people thought of a church as a place where we work together seeking to do the will of God, rather than a place where we meet on Sunday morning. As Christians together we are helping to build something, the Kingdom. We must take the foundation of Jesus Christ and build carefully upon it—not just within our personal lives, but in our world. When Christians are doing this they are truly a church. As Paul repeatedly states, every Christian has a role to play, a gift to give, a work to do.

Scripture: 1 Corinthians 3:10

Device: A small table, some building blocks

Goals: To demonstrate how churches work
To experience working together as Christians

Technique: Ask the children if they have ever played house. Tell them that today everyone is going to play church. Ask if any of them have ever played church. How do they think one plays church? You will get stock answers: by praying, worshiping, singing. Tell the children that Paul wrote a letter in which he talks about how to play church. Read the Scripture and explain how Paul played church: he built things for Jesus. That is how we are going to play church too. We are going to build something for Jesus.

Tell the children that Jesus wants them to build a building with their blocks. But there are rules as to how it is to be done. Each child who wants to play church must take a block, for the children are going to lay the blocks down and make a building. Each child will take a turn and build on top of what the other children have done. Each child must be careful not to knock over what someone else has built. After you have explained the rules, have the children put their blocks in place, each in turn, to build a building. When the children have finished, look at the building that has been constructed. They all played a part. Each child helped build something by working with other children, each adding a block. Have the children take blocks and do it again. Close by stating that when people work together and build something for Jesus they are truly a church.

Notes: Maintain some order or the children will all start building at once. This not only lessens the learning experience but usually results in blocks being knocked over and the building left looking half finished.

BIBLE TRUTHS

38. The Most Beautiful Rock Contest

Theme: Real beauty and goodness come from inside.

One of the tragedies of our culture is its emphasis upon external beauty and external goodness. This type of emphasis discounts those people who do not seem to measure up in their outward appearance. Many people spend their lives trying to be some false, cardboard image of goodness and beauty. Many beautiful people go through life with qualities that are totally missed and unappreciated. A person need not be externally pretty to be truly beautiful. The real prize in many people is inside.

Scripture: Psalm 118:22

Device: Two geodes, one cut in half; several other stones, some prettier than others

Goals: To examine the meaning of beauty
To speak against our culture's false sense of beauty
To support those who do not feel beautiful
To seek signs of hidden beauty

Technique: Place the stones on a table that is covered with a cloth. Have the whole geode with these stones; keep the one that is cut in half in your pocket. The stones should range from plain to pretty; but, for the sake of the lesson, none should outdo the interior of the geode. The children will judge a beauty contest of the stones. After they have chosen, you will pick the whole geode as the prettiest. The outward appearance of the geode is ugly. Inside it is wonderful.

Put a little showmanship into the message. Announce that there will be a beauty contest and the children are to be the judges. It is going to be the world's most beautiful rock contest! Make it fun. With a flourish, unveil the stones to be judged. As you point to each stone the children are to raise their hands or clap their hands if they think that stone is the prettiest. Give them a little time to examine the stones; then have each stone voted on. Keep track of the voting and announce the winner.

After the voting is finished and the winner declared, announce which stone you think is the most beautiful. The geode! The children will wonder why you picked that one; if they don't, then probe a little bit. Ask if they don't really think the geode is the most beautiful. Why do they think the others are prettier? After they have given their reasons, exclaim, "Oh, you're judging by how the stones look on the outside. I was judging by how the stones look on the inside." Then pull out the halved geode to prove your point. Explain that the ugly stone they see on the table is actually like this on the inside, showing them the beautiful colored crystals. Let the children touch the inside of the geode and see it closely. Ask if this really isn't more beautiful than any on the table.

Make your point now: You can't always tell what is prettiest by looking on the outside. Hold the stones up to clarify your point. A lot of people are beautiful and good inside in a way that can't be easily seen. Like the geode, a lot of people who don't look pretty can be very nice. In fact, even if we think we are not very beautiful, we may be like the geode. We may be very beautiful inside. Every single one of us is like this stone, and has some real goodness inside. All we have to do is let it out; let people see how good and pretty we are inside.

Notes: Let the stones, and the geode especially, carry the message. Though you are the one who will be speaking, keep it on a child's level by repeatedly referring to the geode and the stones as examples.

39. Being Humble

Theme: God wants us to be humble.

Humility is a difficult virtue to attain. Our egos feed upon attention, flattery, and achievement, so we seek these things. We bolster ourselves by building ourselves up, often at someone's expense. The virtue of humility, which God desires in us, is self-effacing, not needing other people to prove our worth and goodness. Humility does not degrade either one's self or others. In humble persons, pride has changed into self-respect. They seek to build others up, rather than to broadcast their own successes. God will bless the humble person.

Scripture: James 4:6

Device: An acted demonstration

Goals: To teach the meaning of humility
 To demonstrate conceit and false pride

Technique: The intention of this lesson is to define, by demonstrating false pride, what it means to be humble. You will need to act the part of a bragging, conceited person. Do it in a broadly exaggerated and comical way so that the meaning is clear. The children will be able to understand humility by seeing its opposite.

Ask the children what it means to brag? Children have dealt with individuals who say how good they are, often putting others down at the same time. Do the children like people who brag and say how good they are? God doesn't. God says not to brag or talk about how we are better than someone else. God wants us to be humble instead. Ask if they have heard the word "humble." Do they know what the word means? Many of the children probably do not.

Ask one of the girls to stand up and walk a short distance. After she has done so, walk over to her with an exaggerated swagger, primping your hair along the way, announcing that you are much prettier than she is. Play it for humor; then ask the children which one of you is being humble. They may not understand the first time. Explain that you were bragging, and people who are humble do not brag. Demonstrate again, this time using a boy. Stand next to him, flexing your muscles and emphasizing your tallness. Announce that you are much stronger than the boy. Say this in a conceited way. Again, do it humorously and ask which of you is being humble. By now all the children will know which action is bragging and which is not, which action is humble and which is conceited. State once more that God wants us to be humble persons, not braggarts. God will bless the humble.

Notes: You can use any demonstration of bragging, but act it broadly, aiming for laughs. This will remove the possibility of hurting the child's feelings.

40. Who's on First?

Theme: Nothing is to be more important to us than God in Jesus Christ.

The first of the Ten Commandments is also the most far reaching. It complements the teachings of Christ, in which he states that we cannot serve both God and mammon (Matthew 6:24). If we are honest, we confess that we do find objects that we place before our commitment to the God revealed in Christ.

To discern this about ourselves takes a high degree of integrity and is important for our personal growth as Christians. Objects that commonly come before God in our lives are nation, money, luxuries, family, safety, self.

The First Commandment says that nothing in our lives is to be more important than God. For Christians, this means that nothing is to be more important than the God revealed in Jesus Christ.

Scripture: Exodus 20:3

Device: An American flag, a $5 bill, a common toy, a lipstick, a picture of Jesus

Goals: To educate about Christian values
To evaluate personal values
To encourage making God the most important value

Technique: Ask the children to list some of their favorite things. What do they most like to do? What do they most like to eat? When they have given a good selection, explain the meaning of the First Commandment. The Bible says that we are to like God more than our favorite things. It is all right to like birthday parties, or ice cream, or swimming, but God is more important.

Tell the children that there are things people often like more than God. Hold up the items you have collected, explaining that people sometimes put these things ahead of God. They think these things are greater than God. But the Bible says that God is greater, and is more important than anything else.

Hold up each item and explain it. The flag: People put America ahead of God. They think that being an American is more important than being a Christian. They would rather follow America than follow God. The Bible says this is wrong. The $5 bill: Some people put money ahead of God. They would rather be rich than be Christian. They would rather make money than become good Christians. The Bible says this is wrong. The lipstick: Some people are more concerned about how pretty they look than about God. They pay more attention to their looks than to going to church. The Bible says this is wrong. The toy: Some people are more interested in playing than in loving God and going to church. But the Bible says this is wrong too.

The Bible says that nothing is to be more important than God.

Arrange the objects in a line, placing the picture of Jesus ahead of them all. This is what the First Commandment tells us to do. We are to put God first. If we put God first, and do first what God tells us to do, then we can enjoy all the other things.

Notes: Use your own knowledge of the people in the congregation and portray things that they put ahead of Christ in their lives. It is important to begin a child's education in this difficult area of values

41. Apples and Seeds

Theme: We are to honor our father and mother.

This commandment, first recorded by Moses, is one of those antiquated, out-of-fashion, neglected teachings. In a society where youth is worshiped and old age considered ugly and frightening, this is hardly surprising. Nor does it do any good to oversimplify the difficult situations to which this commandment does not give practical answers. But it is important that this teaching be revived, and the foundation for its meaning communicated.

Scripture: Exodus 20:12

Device: Apple, apple seeds, a knife

Goals: To instill respect for parents
To demonstrate the purpose for the teaching

Technique: Begin with a dialogue centered around the word "honor." Do the children have any idea what the word means? Briefly explain that honor is like respect, especially in terms of actions. To respect people is to look up to them, be good to them, help them, share with them. We are to do this for our parents. Ask the children what they do to honor their parents. Whatever they say, give plenty of positive feedback and support. The children need to know they are doing the right thing.

Ask the children why the Bible would teach us to be good to our parents and help our parents. The children will most likely have some ideas: because their parents made them, or because their parents give them food and clothes and presents.

Use the apple and seeds to demonstrate the purpose for

the teaching. Ask the children what they think might be inside the apple. They will know that there are seeds inside. Cut the apple open and show them. Explain that we are like the seeds and our parents are like the apple. Our parents make us, keep us safe, and help us grow until we are ready to grow all alone. And because they do all that for us, we are to be good to them. Finally, hand each of the children an apple seed and tell them it is to help them remember why they should be good to their parents.

Notes: If you have enough time, have the children list what they can do to help their parents. Have them decide on one or two things to do during the week.

One child asked me where the first apple seed came from.

42. Have You Hugged Your Parents Today?

Theme: We are to respect our father and mother.

Respect is an appropriate word for child/parent relationships, but it is also a cold word. Respect for parents, as Jesus teaches it, involves more than mental appreciation. It involves an actively caring response (Matthew 15:1–9).

Scripture: Exodus 20:12

Device: A chalkboard and a piece of chalk

Goals: To instill respect for parents
To help children express affection for their parents
To improve child/parent relationships

Technique: Ask the children what their mothers and fathers do for them. Use the chalkboard to record what they tell you. Write down everything you have room for. As the children respond, involve them in a discussion. How many of them have parents who do the same things for them? Anything will be helpful that makes clear to the children how much their parents do for them.

After you have an impressive list, ask the children what they do when someone gives them a gift. If someone gave them a piece of candy, what would they say in return? They would say thank you. Ask if they have said thank you to their parents today. If they say yes, ask how they did it. There are different ways of saying thank you: words, hugs, kisses. Make sure the children are aware of the different manners of saying thanks. Help them to understand how to say thanks. If you know all the children and know whether their parents are present, you can ask the children to give their parents a hug right then. Otherwise, tell the children to give their parents a big hug the very next time they see them. Their parents have given them a lot. The right thing for the children to do is to say thanks by giving their parents a hug today.

Notes: This type of suggestion does work. This was done with a group of teenagers I was working with from over a countywide area. I received a phone call from a mother in a town forty miles away. She wanted to thank me for the message we had given to their teenagers. Her daughter had come home that night and given her a hug, which the mother had found very meaningful.

43. Dead Matches

Theme: Death, the end of life, comes to all of us.

Death is an unpleasant subject for most people. We avoid the topic as much as possible, and avoid situations that bring us into contact with it. I even find myself postponing writing on this subject. That is all the more reason to discuss the subject with children. Only rarely will they be taught about death in any formal sense. Only rarely will they discuss the subject with parents, family, or teacher. Children are aware of the fact of death. What they learn they pick up from what they see and hear. This needs to be changed and dealt with by the church.

Scripture: Psalm 89:47–48

Device: A book of matches, an ashtray

Goals: To break the taboo of discussing death
To communicate the universality of death
To teach that death means that life ceases

Technique: A match will be used as the symbol for life and death. A burning match is a visual metaphor for life. The purpose of the match is to allow the children to visualize death in their minds.

Ask the children if any of their pets have ever died. Let them tell you about it. Children will want to talk about the deaths of their pets. These are traumatic events for children which they need to discuss.

After they have told you some stories, ask what happens when an animal dies. What makes it dead? Children have ideas. For our daughter, our mother cat was dead because its breasts didn't work anymore. The ideas expressed are profound learnings for a child. Explain that when a dog is dead its body doesn't work anymore. Its eyes do not see; its nose does not smell; its tail does not wag. It is not alive. This happens to everything, including people. Every single person will die.

Light a match and tell the children that their pets are like your match. With a lighted match, state for the children the comparison between the lighted match and a dog who has been born and is living. As they watch, the match will go out leaving a little trail of smoke. Point out that the dog dies and isn't alive anymore. Sometimes our pet gets run over by a car. Then (lighting a match) the pet is like a burning match that is blown out. Blow the match out and watch the smoke rise. Light another match, holding it upright between your fingers, letting it go out naturally. This match is like a person. The person is born, lives, and dies. All people die.

Hold up a burned-out match. This is what a dead body is like, whether it is a dog, cat, or person. It can't work anymore. The match won't light anymore. Someday we all will be like this. Our bodies will die and no longer work. Light a new match, telling them that today we all are alive. Blow out the match and tell the children that someday we all will die—until the day God brings us all back to life.

Notes: Don't avoid this lesson or this subject. Children need to learn about death, especially in the context of Christianity.

Examine your own discomfort in dealing with this subject.

If you hold a lighted match between your fingers, the match will extinguish itself before burning you. It may relieve some of your anxieties if you test this out.

It may also relieve some of your anxiety to know that this lesson did not scare or sadden any of the children with whom I spoke. They exhibited interest and a certain amount of detachment regarding the subject. Children have a natural curiosity about death; however, it is not completely real for them yet.

44. Day for Rest

Theme: Sunday is to be a day of rest, dedicated to God.

How much healthier people and families would be if they truly took a day of rest once a week. Work all week, work all weekend, run, dash, pant, collapse, start again. That's not what the Lord had in mind. Clergy can be just as self-destructive, working seven days a week, thinking they are doing the Lord's will the whole time. This command says otherwise. We are not to become pharisaic about the Sabbath: can't cook, can't play, can't go places. For clergy and some other people, Sunday can't be the nonworking day. But for most people, Sunday is to be a day of rest centered around worship of God and time with family. It is a day to give thanks, relax, and have fun—if you know how to have fun. If not, ask the children; they know.

Scripture: Exodus 20:8–10

Device: A game

Goals: To experience the difference between busyness and rest

To explore the meaning of the Sabbath Day

To teach that it is all right to rest

Technique: After reading the Scripture to the children, give them a brief explanation of what God had in mind. God made the world in six days and on the seventh day he rested. He tells us to do the same. Now you are ready to put the children through their paces.

Ask them all to stand and run in place. Demonstrate for them, so that all will know what you mean. Take a few moments to have them all run with you, then stop. Explain that you are now going to have them run through a normal week. Tell them to start running because it is Monday and they have to get to school. After a few moments tell them it is Tuesday and there is still school, so they must keep running. After several more moments it is Wednesday, but they keep running because school meets on Wednesday too. Do the same for Thursday and Friday. On Saturday they have to run because they have to work around the house and they have a ball game to play. Finally, declare that it is Sunday and that all can sit. As all breathe easier, explain that this is what Sunday is to be like. It is to be a break from what they do the rest of the week. It is a time to rest, to go to church and worship God. Have the children repeat their running in place. Tell them you are going to have them go through another week. This time, as you go through the week, add some different touches. As they run on Tuesday, have them wave their arms in circles. Or as they run on Wednesday, have them run in small circles. Use your imagination. Finally, on Sunday, have the children sit down once more. God tells us to relax and worship him on Sunday. He wants us to go to church and be with our family, things we may not do the rest of the week. Sunday is to be our day for rest.

Notes: Hope you are in shape for this lesson!

All those people who work on Sunday need to take another day for the same reasons.

45. Gossip

Theme: We are not to gossip.

Talking about other people, behind their backs, seems to be a natural human activity. But the Bible counsels us not to indulge in gossip. It is a sure way to arouse anger, lose friends, make enemies, spread dissension, and broadcast falsehood.

Scripture: Proverbs 25:23

Device: A dialogue

Goals: To experience what gossip is
To demonstrate its harmfulness

Technique: This sermon picks up on the tremendous interest human beings have in the lives of other people. It is this interest which leads to gossip. You will be amazed at how quickly children become involved.

Ask the children if they have heard the word "gossip." Do they know what it means? They probably will have some concept of it, reflecting what they have heard around their home. Discuss gossip with them: what it does, the Bible's teaching about it. Emphasize the anger it can arouse and the falsehoods it can spread. This is why the Bible tells us not to gossip.

After a short discussion remark to the children, "Oh, by the way, did I tell you who Brian's latest girl friend is?" Whisper a name to a girl in the group. Ask if anyone else wants to know. There will be many giggles, and everyone will want to know, while Brian has fits. Before you finish passing on this choice information, ask if the children heard the naughty thing Sue did. No one has, of course. Make something up and whisper it in a boy's ear. Ask if anyone else wants to know. Now their interest is definitely aroused.

Conclude by asking what you have been doing. You have been talking about Brian and Sue, without Brian and Sue being able to hear what you say. This is gossip. The Bible says not to gossip. It can cause other people to be angry; it can spread lies. Point out to the children that nothing you told them about Brian or Sue was true. That's what gossip is like, and God says never to gossip about other people.

Notes: Pick any two children from the group to be the subjects of your gossip.

For the surest response, when gossiping about a boy whisper to a girl, and when gossiping about a girl whisper to a boy.

46. What Do You Do with a Bible?

Theme: The Bible is meant to be read.

Being God's written word, the Bible is meant to be read and studied as part of our daily life. In this way God can speak to us through the Scriptures. But he can speak to us in this way only if we do read and study his Scriptures. The Bible is of little use to those who rarely open its cover.

Scripture: Acts 17:11

Device: A Bible

Goals: To teach the purpose of the Bible

To teach how to use the Bible

To encourage Bible-reading

Technique: Hold up a Bible, asking the children what is in your hand. What is a Bible used for? Where is it used? After a brief discussion with them, open the Bible, displaying the written pages, and ask what a Bible is? It's a book. Books are full of words, and this book is full of God's words. What do we do with a book? After their answer, pretend you do not believe them. Hold the Bible to your ear. Can we hear a book? Sit on the Bible. Can we sit on the Bible and know what it says? Use your imagination. Place the book under a candlestick. Can a Bible talk to us from underneath a candlestick? Lay the Bible down and order it to talk. Can a Bible talk out loud? The children will respond with a chorus of no's. Again, ask, What do we do with a book? A book is meant to be read. We have to read the words. Point out that the people in the book of Acts studied the Bible; they read it. The Bible is meant for us to read. When we read the

Bible we will read God's words. Encourage the children to read the Bible too. When they do, God will speak to them through the book.

47. Lock and Key

Theme: The Bible can solve the tough problems in life.

The Bible is important for what it teaches us and also for the opportunity it gives for Christ to speak to us. The Bible can unlock the toughest problems; it can undo the toughest knots. If we take our problems to the Bible, the Bible will answer our deepest questions and talk to us about the mysteries. In a life full of many locked doors, the Bible is a key.

Scripture: 2 Timothy 3:15

Device: A padlock and key

Goals: To teach a purpose for the Bible
To demonstrate that purpose
To help children know that the Bible is for them too

Technique: Hold up a Bible and ask the children what you have in your hands. When they have answered, ask them what a Bible is. This will give you an indication of what the children know and think. It will also start them thinking about the Bible. Ask: How many read in the Bible? How many have Bibles? Have a dialogue with the children about it.

Ask the children to list when the Bible is used. Why do people read it? The children may be able to think of nothing more than that it is read in church. Tell them you know another way to use the Bible; you can use it to solve problems. Not math types of problems, but problems with life and people. What do you do when a person picks on you? The Bible will tell you. What happens after you die? Again, the Bible deals with that question. The Bible will tell you who made the world, and you and me. Ask the children who made the world. After they respond "God," emphasize that they are right and they learned that from the Bible. If they have a tough problem, they can use the Bible to find an answer.

Take the padlock and fasten it to one of the children, on a piece of the child's clothing. A good place is around the belt loop on a boy's pants. Ask the boy if he can remove the lock. Ask the other children. When they have given up, tell them that only a key will open the padlock so it can be removed. Hold up the key. Explain that the Bible is like a key. It will help us solve problems we can't deal with by ourselves. Unlock the padlock and repeat: The Bible is a key to problems in life.

Notes: If you fasten the padlock to a belt loop, don't let the child tear off the belt loop in an effort to remove the lock.

LOVE OF SELF AND OTHERS

48. Hurray for Me

Theme: We are to love ourselves.

The Golden Rule of Jesus Christ has two parts: Love your neighbor as you love yourself. One of the parts, loving yourself, has been all but forgotten. Loving ourselves is often regarded as wrong or egotistical, but nothing could be farther from the truth. Jesus gives us permission to love ourselves. Loving ourselves will not cause us to love other people less; it will help us to love others more. What Jesus says is more than a command. It is fact. We love other people exactly as we love ourselves.

Scripture: Mark 12:31

Device: A dialogue

Goals: To explain to the children that we are to love ourselves

To communicate the importance of self-love

To build self-esteem

Technique: After reading the Scripture, state to the children that Jesus says we are to love ourselves. We often think of Christianity as meaning we must love other people. We are also to love ourselves.

Ask the children what they do well. Have them tell you something they are proud of, or feel good about, or have accomplished. These things may not pour out of them. You may have to be patient, prod a little. Ask them individually what they do well. If you have some prior knowledge or ideas, and if the children are bashful, point out to them what you know they do well.

Even at their early age they may have learned already not to speak well of themselves. They will probably be reticent or will feel embarrassed to share publicly any good word about themselves. They may even think they are not good at anything and have no talent or gifts. You can ask if they love themselves. Ask them this individually. You hope someone will say yes. But most will look at you bashfully, or even say no.

After you have the children share what they do well (share, play, keep their room clean, take care of brother), ask them to say, "Hurray for me!" Since they do all these good things, they certainly deserve to cheer for themselves. They will probably be reticent about this too. If they refuse or only partially respond, you will have to enlist the help of the congregation. Ask the people to say, "Hurray for me!" I found the choir most helpful. The choir members responded en masse, making it easier for the children. Have everybody repeat the phrase a few times, saying it louder each time. Challenge the people to yell it as loud as possible. Have the entire congregation join in saying the phrase, "Hurray for me!"

Notes: This sermon works directly on one of the most limiting aspects of human life, a poor self-image. The feeling of the whole congregation picks up, noticeably, after the chorus of hurrays. Follow it with a joyous song.

49. Teddy Bears

Theme: Love is openness to others.

While we hold forth love as the greatest of emotions, few people understand love or practice it well. We are taught that love is a feeling of attraction, or sex. We confuse needing to be loved with loving others. We are taught that love is an ideal not realizable in the real world. There is need to educate ourselves and our children to the truth about love, counteracting the lies of our world.

Part of the scary nature of love, and what gives it idealistic color, is love's openness. Love is open to all, not closed, even to enemies. Christ upon the cross is the ultimate example of love's openness: physically, mentally, emotionally, and spiritually. In openness we accept all people, making ourselves vulnerable. In this lie both fear and love.

Scripture: John 15:12

Device: A teddy bear

Goals: To educate about the meaning of love
To demonstrate love as openness
To support a child's natural openness
To encourage loving

Technique: A teddy bear is a perfect example of openness. The classic teddy bear is made in an inviting position, arms and legs extended, open to any who would hold it. Without question, this posture has much to do with its appeal, along with its being very warm, furry, and huggable.

Ask the children who loves them. How do they know? You will get all sorts of answers, many about being nice, kind, helpful. In fact, children know more about love than do most adults.

After they have talked, ask them how many have teddy bears. Do they sleep with them? Do they take them places? How many of the children love their teddy bears? Have them raise their hands. Pull out your own teddy bear and give it a big hug. Ask if yours is like theirs. Explain that teddy bears are very loving animals; they are always willing to give us a hug. No matter how bad we've been, no matter how mean, teddy bears will always hug us. Ask how a teddy bear holds its arms. Have the children show you. When our arms are like that, we are always ready for a hug. The teddy bear's arms are open, ready for some loving.

That's what love is like. Love is like a teddy bear. Love's arms are always open, ready to hug someone, no matter who. Love is open; it is inviting. How many have ever seen a teddy bear with its arms folded across its chest? Show the children what you mean. Is that type of teddy bear ready to hug? No, it's not. And that's not love. Ask if any of them would like a hug. If they don't come running to you, go give them hugs.

Notes: This lesson gives you a chance to express some physical affection. When your arms are open, demonstrate by hugging one of them. At the end give some more hugs. If you have rapport with the children, some will undoubtedly respond. Many of the children need positive strokes—perhaps badly. If you can give those strokes, you will have accomplished more than words could ever say.

50. The Specialness Game

Theme: Everyone is special and important in a particular, unique way.

A requirement for self-love is knowing how you are important, different, and worthwhile. A sense of self-worth is necessary for any amount of self-esteem and self-love to exist. Psalm 8 tells us how important and unique we are in creation. Each person is different from everyone else. Each person has something no one else has. This makes every individual special, worthwhile, and worth loving.

Scripture: Psalm 8

Device: A game

Goals: To help the children discover how they are special
To build a sense of self-worth
To support a sense of self-love

Technique: The goal of the game is to demonstrate each person's uniqueness. This is done by eliminating persons, using certain criteria, until only one person is left standing. For example: Begin by asking all the boys to sit. This leaves only the girls standing. Ask all who are right-handed to sit. This leaves only left-handed girls standing. Ask all the remaining girls who are in third grade or higher to sit. This leaves only left-handed girls below third grade standing. Continue this process until only one girl is left. No matter what the criteria you have used, the girl left standing is unique in her own way. She may be the only left-handed girl below third grade in the church. This makes her different, important, special, and worthwhile. Repeat this game as often as you wish, aiming to show how different persons are special.

When you have narrowed a playing of the game down to only one person, be sure to enumerate the qualities that make this person special. Explain how everyone is special in some way. If you had time, you could do this game for everyone present. Individuality makes each person important, for each one has something no one else has.

Notes: This sermon works well if you have a large group of children.

If there are some children you want to support by demonstrating their uniqueness and specialness, choose criteria that will leave only those children standing.

Don't be embarrassed if you choose something that makes everyone sit. Just choose something else.

LOVE OF JESUS

51. JIMF

Theme: Jesus is our friend.

One of the most down-to-earth, daily experiences of love from others is friendship. When we speak about friendship, everyone knows what we mean. A person's friends may be few, but they are precious. Jesus says that he is our friend. That is an expression of love very practical and easy to understand.

Scripture: John 15:15

Device: Enough tags with the letters JIMF on them to give one to each child

Goals: To teach that Jesus loves each child as a friend
To encourage each child to feel loved
To cultivate a sense of self-worth

Technique: After you read the Scripture, have the children talk about friendship. How many of them have friends? What makes someone a friend? Do the children do things together? Do they help each other? Dialogue about friendship, moving the children into a discussion about the dynamics of friendship.

Whatever the children say about friendship, apply it to Jesus. Jesus says he is our friend. He is all the things just mentioned. Jesus helps us, spends time with us. He likes to be with us, if we want to be with him. He's with us right now, right here. He's beside each of us. Jesus likes us. He's our friend.

Give each of the children a JIMF tag. Ask if anyone knows what the letters stand for. They stand for "Jesus Is My Friend." Have the children wear the tags. The tags are to remind them that Jesus is their friend, no matter where they are.

Notes: The tags can be fastened on the children with tape or with string, like a necklace. The tags themselves can be made of construction paper, with the letters written on. If possible, have the children make the tags themselves, without telling them what the letters mean. Leave them in suspense until you reveal it as part of the lesson.

INDEX

Scripture Passages

.